T0063154

Immanuel Moments

STEVE WHEELER

WESTBOW
PRESS
A DIVISION OF THOMAS NELSON

WestBow Press books may be ordered through booksellers or by contacting:

WestBow Press
A Division of Thomas Nelson
1663 Liberty Drive
Bloomington, IN 47403
www.westbowpress.com
1-(866) 928-1240

Because of the dynamic nature of the Internet, any web addresses or links contained in this book may have changed since publication and may no longer be valid. The views expressed in this work are solely those of the author and do not necessarily reflect the views of the publisher, and the publisher hereby disclaims any responsibility for them.

All Scripture taken from the English Standard Version (ESV) unless otherwise noted

Any people depicted in stock imagery provided by Thinkstock are models, and such images are being used for illustrative purposes only.

Certain stock imagery © Thinkstock.

ISBN: 978-1-4497-8711-0 (sc)
ISBN: 978-1-4497-8713-4 (hc)
ISBN: 978-1-4497-8712-7 (e)

Library of Congress Control Number: 2013904037

Printed in the United States of America

WestBow Press rev. date: 03/21/2013

Also by
Steve Wheeler
Forget What? The Philippian Misconception

To all of those who encouraged me to write … again
To all of those who are in tough situations,
may you find words of encouragement within these pages

Contents

Preface

In 2009, I self-published my first book, *Forget What? The Philippian Misconception*. The central theme of that book was a misconception that had been created by a misinterpretation of Paul's words found in Philippians 3:13–14: "Brothers, I do not consider that I have made it my own. But one thing I do: forgetting what lies behind and straining forward to what lies ahead, I press on toward the goal for the prize of the upward call of God in Christ Jesus." The misconception is that we are to forget about the past with all of its pain, heartache, and guilt and look to the future. The truth is we are not called to forget the events from our historical past, but rather we are to forget all of the things that we put our trust in to be right with God and look upward to Christ alone for our salvation. Once the truth is seen about the past, I then talk about dealing with the past. *Forget What? The Philippian Misconception* is a book that talks about taking those events from the past that hinder us and instead use them for the glory of God and the good of mankind.

Over the past three years, several people that have read my first book asked when I was going to write again. I acted like I was working on some ideas but was having a tough time writing. In reality, I had reached a point where I felt like I was no longer connected to God; thus, no words were available to write.

In August of 2012 things changed quickly. One friend began texting me song titles and messages that spoke to the fact that God was starting a "new thing" in my life. One of her emails spoke of a new book I was about to write, a book that talked about the things God had done throughout my life. Within the next forty-eight hours, four more people requested the second book, the follow-up book to the first. Two of those people used the word *sequel*. The confirmation to write was there.

Immanuel Moments consists of three major sections: the introduction, three sermon outlines, and thirty-one personal stories. The introduction tells how my life was changed through a song and several emails, thus leading me to write the manuscript. The three sermons, "Immanuel Moments," "Stones of Remembrance," and "Spiritual Pep Talks," talk about the miraculous power of God in the midst of His people, the manner in which He brought them through the circumstances they faced, and the encouragement and hope that can be found in remembering those events for generations to come. In the thirty-one personal stories, I talk about different times and aspects of my life in which God revealed Himself to me in an unusual way. To demonstrate His presence, I share stories that talk about events before I came to know Christ, events after I came to know Christ, the living Word coming to life, hearing His voice, dreams that He shared with me, and healings He performed for me. *Immanuel Moments* is about God doing uncommon things in the lives of common people. *Immanuel Moments* is about *God*.

In *Forget What? The Philippian Misconception,* I talk about reclaiming those past events from our lives that haunt us and beat us down. I encourage others to tell those stories that demonstrate the power of God in our lives in order to encourage others so they, too, can be set free.

Immanuel Moments carries that concept one step further in that I share stories taken from my life that demonstrate how God does uncommon things in the lives of common people. It doesn't stop there, however. Several people who have read the manuscript and have heard me talk about it want to share their stories to help encourage others too. *Immanuel Moments II* would contain more sermon outlines of God's supernatural presence in the lives of His people, along with real stories from other people who have experienced their own Immanuel moments.

Special thanks to …
Tamra Garman and Steve Leach,
for being faithful friends and messengers.
Johnna Gonzales and Sarah Guthrie,
for edits of the manuscript.
Luke Wheeler,
for his input in the final cover selection.
And of course,
Immanuel—God with me—
for all of the powerful things He has done in my life!

Introduction

"Gloom, despair, and agony on me. Deep, dark depression, excessive misery. If it weren't for bad luck, I'd have no luck at all. Gloom, despair, and agony on me."[1] Such were the words sang by four sulking hillbillies on the television show *Hee Haw*. After singing through the chorus the first time, each one of the four men would share a part of their story of sadness and woe. Once they were done talking, they would sing their chorus again. The scene would fade away with all four men sobbing like babies on each other's shoulders.

While they sang their songs of gloom, despair, and agony for entertainment, many of us can sing that same song from our reality. While their stories of sadness and woe were quite comical, almost to the point of pure nonsense, our stories are true and serious. Our stories involve sickness, disease, addictions, broken relationships, lost jobs, and poverty, to name but a few. Our stories cast dark shadows over our lives, blocking out any ray of hope for a better tomorrow. There seems to be no end in sight as we walk through the darkest periods of our lives.

In 2011 I entered into the darkest period of my life. I found myself physically, mentally, and emotionally exhausted. I had reached a point spiritually where I no longer felt close to God. In fact, the thoughts that ruled my mind said that I had overstepped my boundaries, and that God had utterly rejected me. I was quickly burning out and near extinction. In August of 2012 I sent an email of desperation to three of my most trusted friends.

In that email I told my friends that I knew how Adam felt when he was driven from the presence of God and banished from the garden. I knew how Jonah felt when he was taken to the darkest depths of the sea inside the guts of the great fish. I knew how Sampson felt when he was blinded, fettered, and forced to slave away in the obscure gristmill of the Philistine prison. I knew how the outcast of the Corinthian letters must have felt when he was banished from the fellowship. I understood the words of Psalm 51 like never before, especially the cry, "Cast me not away from your presence, and take not your Holy Spirit from me."

If that's not the cry of a desperate heart, I don't know what is. Naturally, as I knew they would, my friends contacted me with words of encouragement. I cherish every word they wrote and spoke, along with the prayers that they have prayed over me. At this point, all I could do was wait upon the Lord.

About a year ago, I reconnected with a friend I had not seen in forty years. Up to this point, our conversations had been casual. I had not told her anything about myself or my situation that would prompt her to do what she did on August 11 and in the days that followed. It started with a link to a song called "It's Not Over" by Ricardo Sanchez.[2] I listened to the song a couple of times. I wrote to my friend and said, "Very timely and needed. So … what prompted you to share that out of the blue?" Her response floored me. She wrote back and said, "Don't have time to put it in the right words yet. Need to listen some more to Holy Spirit before I say. Listening is something

I am working on. Has something to do with the beginning of your new book and a miracle that will bring thousands into the Kingdom of God. A double dog dare for you. A suddenly that's going to shake your world, Mister."

Over the course of the next few weeks my friend sent me several emails and texts with very explicit instructions. Sometimes she would share a passage of Scripture. Other times she would share links to songs or sermons I needed to read or hear. She said she had more to share, but that would come in time. She sent one email that she immediately instructed me to delete before reading, but I had already read it. One line in the email spoke about putting my testimony in writing. I had already put a lot of my life into my first book, but she seemed to imply there was more.

Over the weekend I grabbed my laptop and started writing. It needs to be noted that apart from sermons I have written, from the time I finished my first book in 2009 to the present, I could not write. Every time I sat down at a computer or a notepad, my mind would go blank. It was frustrating, because I wanted to write. In less than one hour that weekend, I had the title, the format, the headings, and a working outline completed for the book. Before the weekend was over, I had typed five thousand words.

A few days later I had an encounter with a client at work who had purchased a copy of my first book. He had read it several times and liked it. Each time he came in the office he would ask about my second book. I would always play it down by telling him I was working on a few subjects. On this particular day he had left the office but turned around and came back in with a serious look on his face. Without any provocation he asked, "When do I get my book?" I said, "You already have one." His expression was very straight, not his usual smile, and he said, "Not that one; the new one! You are a gifted writer, and I've read the first one several times, and it's very inspirational. But I was wondering where the follow-up book was. I feel like there should have been more. Are you not going to tell me more?" I jokingly asked him, "Are you talking about a sequel?" He replied, "Tell me the rest of the story."

The next day was the same thing. Within the first hour of work, a client's conversation turned to talking about my Christian life. She wanted to know why I hadn't written a second book. When I tried to explain that I had hit a wall, having nothing to say or write, she was insistent that I had not been listening. I tried to explain that I needed to get the wellspring cleared out so the deep things could start flowing again, but she kept telling me I was not listening. I assured her that I was now listening and that the next book would be out very soon.

Right before lunch a woman brought her daughter in for services, and since the clinic was closed for lunch, we had time to talk. I knew from a previous encounter that the mother had been through a jet-skiing accident where she broke several bones. That in itself got us to talking about living through difficult situations. Due to an accident in which I lost my right arm, people often ask about my left-handed writing skills. I always tell people that it is a God-given gift that my hand works so well. She told her daughter to ask how I lost my arm—the mom already knew. When I finished the details, her mom looked at her and said that I was proof God still performs miracles. The mother told me that I should tell that story more often, because people need to know that God is still at work.

Later that afternoon I received a phone call from another client who had bought a copy of my first book. He, too, was always asking about my next book. When I answered the phone, he started his conversation with, "Steve, this is Ron. Do you remember me? When do I get a copy of your next book? I'm ready for more." I told him I was in the process of writing the next one even as we spoke. He was pleased. Then he said, "I have a friend in Dallas who often does free editing as a ministry. I'll hook you up if you want me to." Naturally, I said I would keep that in mind.

After I hung up the phone, my coworker turned around and apologized for eavesdropping. She then proceeded to inform me that her degree includes media editing and that she would be happy to edit my book as well. I asked her how much she would charge. She smiled and said she would be willing to do it for free. Two free editors in five minutes!

The following weekend I found myself tired of writing. My mind was blank and in need of rest to listen for the next direction. In one Saturday morning, I had waded through a large number of photographs I had taken of the sky. I love taking pictures of the horizon, especially when it has brilliant colors. Within a couple of hours, I had created four book covers from pictures I had taken. I then posted them on Facebook, giving my friends the opportunity to tell me which cover caught their attention. The rough draft of the cover was now done.

In five weeks, I went from being mentally drained and unable to write a single word to having typed over thirty-one thousand words. The rough draft was complete and on its way to my friend for editing. My front cover was designed, and all I needed to do was pick the final cover. The back cover of the book was complete as well. All things were falling into place. That is a moment in time when the light of God's presence began breaking through the darkness and despair. That is what I call an Immanuel moment—a moment when I know God is with me.

The name Immanuel means "God with us." Immanuel moments are those times when I know that God is present in my darkest situations. This book is a culmination of sermons and stories that demonstrate the fact that God wants to break through the gloom and despair of our hopeless situations with His miracle-working presence. He wants to be present in the good times and the bad. He wants to enter into our difficult situations and do the impossible. He wants to do far more for us than we could ever ask or think.

In the following pages, I share three messages that demonstrate the Immanuel moment concept of God being in the midst of our darkest times. I finish the book with several stories from my personal life that demonstrate the fact that God is not distant, but actively working in our lives. I share stories that took place before I came to Christ, as well as stories that took place after my conversion. I share the stories before my conversion to show that God is constantly at work in our lives even when we don't want Him there. He does this to draw us to Himself. I share stories following my conversion to show that He continues working in our lives from the time we are converted until we pass from this life into eternity.

Please keep this thought in the forefront of your mind as you read through these stories: They are not, in any way, to bring glory and praise to myself, but rather to bring glory and praise to the One who has given His life for me, who has worked out so many situations that neither I nor anyone else could work out. These stories are told to point you toward Immanuel—God with us.

Section I
Sermon Outlines

In this section, I share three sermon outlines: "Immanuel Moments," "Stones of Remembrance," and "Spiritual Pep Talks." Each outline brings out the concept that God is dwelling in the midst of His people, and He desires to demonstrate His power in every circumstance of life. "Immanuel Moments" tells the story of when Israel needed help in the middle of a desperate situation, and God used the name Immanuel as the promise of His divine deliverance. "Stones of Remembrance" tells of the faithfulness of God to bring His people into the Land of Promise. "Spiritual Pep Talks" is the story of how David used past events to encourage himself in a current situation. All three outlines reveal Immanuel moments, moments in time when God was among His people.

Immanuel Moments

This message is based on two passages of Scripture: Isaiah 7:1–16, which contains the actual prophecy of God's abiding presence, and 2 Kings 16, which is the historical narrative of the events that prompted the prophecy. As we walk through the verses found in Isaiah, I point out a few key verses and make some brief comments.

The Situation: "In the days of Ahaz the son of Jotham, son of Uzziah, king of Judah, Rezin the king of Syria and Pekah the son of Remaliah the king of Israel came up to Jerusalem to wage war against it, but could not yet mount an attack against it. When the house of David was told, "Syria is in league with Ephraim," the heart of Ahaz and the heart of his people shook as the trees of the forest shake before the wind" (Isaiah 7:1-2)

The nation of Israel had divided into two kingdoms—Israel to the north and Judah to the south. Jerusalem, the City of David, was in Judah. Israel and Aram had already attacked parts of Judah, at one point killing over 120,000 valiant men. Now they were marching on the city of Jerusalem in order to divide and conquer. The city was under attack from both foreign powers and its own people from the nation of Israel. Because the two armies could not mount a direct attack on the city, they chose the ancient tactic of building a siege wall around the city to stop the inward flow of supplies. This tactic slowly crushes the inhabitants of the city into surrender and defeat. It's like slowly tightening a noose around one's neck.

There are times when we feel like the enemy has built a wall around our lives, and everything has stopped flowing in. We feel drained, weak, and empty. Doom and destruction are imminent. We then feel like caving in to the pressures of life. We are talking about those times that cause our hearts to shake and tremble like trees in the wind. We are talking about those times when the pressures of life give us the cold sweats at night and hand-wringing during the day. We are talking about those times when we want to bury our heads in the sand or pull a blanket over our heads, hoping the problem will simply go away or change on its own. But it doesn't.

God's message to His people: And the LORD said to Isaiah, "Go out to meet Ahaz, you and Shear-jashub your son, at the end of the conduit of the upper pool on the highway to the Washer's Field. And say to him, 'Be careful, be quiet, do not fear, and do not let your heart be faint because of these two smoldering stumps of firebrands, at the fierce anger of Rezin and Syria and the son of Remaliah. (Isaiah 7:3-4)

It is in those desperate times when we feel all alone and hopeless that the Lord Himself sends His designated person into the situation with a specific word for us. No offense here, but I am not talking about good friends and family members who come to us with a myriad of generic advice, cute clichés, and power statements. I am talking about someone who has heard the voice of God and comes with the answer for our particular situation. In this case, God sent His prophet Isaiah, who appeared to the trembling King Ahaz with a simple three-point sermon: "Take heed ... Be quiet ... Fear Not" (Isaiah 7:4 KJV)

Take heed. Look around and observe your surroundings. Take stock of your situation. Know your enemy, yourself, and your source of supply. Keep your eyes open for the solution. First Corinthians 10:13 states that "no testing has overtaken you that is not common to everyone. God is faithful, and he will not let you be tested beyond your strength, but with the testing he will also provide the way out so that you may be able to endure it."

Be quiet. Psalm 46:10 states, "Be still and know that I am God." Rather than running off to talk to everyone else, we need to learn to wait quietly for the Lord. When faced with troubles in this high-tech world we live in, we will tweet about it, Facebook it, text it, or email it. Sometimes we just need to stop talking. Rather than running off to talk to everyone else or network about it, we need to quietly wait for the Lord, because He sees and hears us in secret and will reward us openly.

Fear not. Fear is the opposite of faith. Fear is allowing Satan to rob us of the faith or hope that something good, that is not yet seen, can occur in our lives. Fear asks the question, "Do you really think God will do that for you?" Hebrews 11:6 states, "Without faith it is impossible to please God, for whoever would approach Him must believe that He exists and that He will reward those who diligently seek him out."

God's view of the adversary and the problem: "And say to him, 'Be careful, be quiet, do not fear, and do not let your heart be faint because of these two smoldering stumps of firebrands, at the fierce anger of Rezin and Syria and the son of Remaliah" (Isaiah 7:4).

The imagery God uses to describe Jerusalem's adversaries is that of a used-up torch. There is no fire, no glow, no heat—only smoke. Imagine a burned-out campfire. There is always one stick that lies there smoking. It has no flame or heat; it only smokes.

Growing up on a farm, it was easy to see where the cows had been after a grass fire had passed through, because you would see all these little plumes of smoke going up. You have to check out hot spots so there will be no rekindling of a fire, only to discover they are nothing more than smoking cow pies! You can pour water on those things, and they will still smoke for days. There is no flame, no heat, no glow—only smoke. God saw the adversaries as nothing more than used-up and powerless smoking cow pies!

God's view of the outcome: "It shall not stand, and it shall not come to pass" (Isaiah 1:7). Yes, the adversary is real. Yes, the attack is approaching, but is the situation hopeless? No! For God says that it shall not stand or come to pass. In Isaiah 54:17 we read, "No weapon that is fashioned against you shall succeed, and you shall refute every tongue that rises against you in judgment. This is the heritage of the servants of the LORD and their vindication from me, declares the LORD."

The catch: "If you do not stand firm in faith, you shall not stand at all." There is always a catch. There is always fine print in every contract. The catch is that we must not shrink back into fear but remain faithful to the hope we have been given. Hebrews 10:23 states, "Let us hold fast the profession of our faith without wavering; for He is faithful that promised." James 1:5–8 states, "If any of you lacks wisdom [I assume we could insert any need here], let him ask God, who gives generously to all without reproach, and it will be given him. But let him ask in faith, with no doubting, for the one who doubts is like a wave of the sea that is driven and tossed by the wind. For that person must not suppose that he will receive anything from the

Lord; he is a double-minded man, unstable in all his ways." We must walk in faith, for that pleases God.

The promise: "Again the LORD spoke to Ahaz, saying, 'Ask a sign of the LORD your God; let it be deep as Sheol or high as heaven.' But Ahaz said, 'I will not ask, and I will not put the LORD to the test.' Then Isaiah said: 'Hear then, O house of David! Is it too little for you to weary mortals, that you weary my God also?'" (vv. 10–13).

Because the king needed an immediate resolution to a pressing problem, God would allow Ahaz to ask for any sign as evidence that He was involved in the situation and everything would work out as He promised. Out of pride, Ahaz refused the opportunity, so God gave His own sign. Isaiah then said in verses 14–16, "Therefore the Lord himself will give you a sign. Look, the young woman is with child and shall bear a son, and shall name him Immanuel. He shall eat curds and honey by the time he knows how to refuse the evil and choose the good. For before the child knows how to refuse the evil and choose the good, the land before whose two kings you are in dread will be deserted." While scholars cannot agree on to whom the "young maiden" refers in this particular passage, they do agree it makes reference to the fact that a young woman is pregnant and close to giving birth, and that before the child is weaned, the problem will be resolved. Some scholars agree that the young child referenced here is Isaiah's son, who was mentioned in verse 3 as living illustration. Bottom line—the resolution was coming fast!

I would like to say that Ahaz embraced all that the prophet said. But he refused to trust God and ran to Assyria for help. Assyria did defeat Syria and Israel and eventually took Judah captive. He was not established, because he did not believe.

How does this apply to you and me? Today, you and I live in the midst of our besieging moments. The events of life seem to surround us, press in on us, and drain us of the joy of life. We find ourselves in dire need, and we look in every direction for relief. Nothing is there. In the midst of our situation, we too, like King Ahaz of old, have been given a sign of deliverance—a child who is called Immanuel—God with us. Through this child we find deliverance from our besieging moments.

This child was born over two thousand years ago in a tiny little town of no significance, and to poor, unknown parents. He grew into full stature and presented Himself as the Son of God, who came to seek and save that which is lost. He came to set captives free. He became the Lamb of God, who was slain for our salvation. That child defeated the powers of hell that seek to kill, steal, and destroy; and He is now seated at the right hand of God, where He is interceding in our behalf. That child is Immanuel—God with us.

If I could give each one of you a gift today, it would be an Immanuel moment. I would give you a moment in time when you know that God has entered into your personal situation. I would give you a time when you know that God is present to deliver you from your besieging moment. I would give you a time when God has done great things in your behalf. These are the moments when you know the reason why things worked out was not luck, or fate, or coincidence, or the work of your own hands. These are the moments when the eternal God of all creation has stepped into your world and things worked out for you!

Stones of Remembrance

The children of Israel were no strangers to the miraculous power of God. Following many signs and wonders performed by the Lord, they were free to walk away from four hundred years of Egyptian bondage. A few days later they found themselves in a dangerous situation with rugged mountains on each side, the armies of Egypt bearing down upon them, and the Red Sea before them. With a pillar of fire between the Israelites and the Egyptians, the Lord prepared a highway of deliverance as He parted the Red Sea, making a way of escape. After they crossed to safety, the fire lifted, allowing the Egyptians to pursue them. The Egyptians met their demise as the walls of water crashed down upon them, destroying the entire army. During their journey to Sinai, the Israelites received manna from heaven for food, water flowing from rocks, and the Lord's covering for protection.

Although accustomed to the miraculous powers of God, the children of Israel were also accustomed to having a short memory. Shortly after they received the Law and the tablets at Sinai, the Lord brought them to the banks of the Jordan River. Twelve spies were sent to Canaan to get the lay of the land, to see what resources the land possessed, and to discover what armies lay before them. All twelve returned to the people with an abundance of resources and a report that it was a land flowing with milk and honey. While Joshua and Caleb were ready to lead the people to a great victory in the land of promise, the ten other spies spoke of giants in the land that were impossible to defeat. The children of Israel forgot the awesome miracles of God and turned away from the land of great provision.

For the next forty years the children of Israel wandered in the wilderness until all of the men of war who refused the Lord's command to possess the land had perished from the earth. A new generation of Israelites stood on the banks of the Jordan River. Once again the people were confronted with the command to cross the river and take possession of the land that flowed with milk and honey, a land with a bountiful supply of resources guarded by the giants that lived there. However, there was a difference in this generation. Forty years earlier ten spies turned the hearts of the people to doubt the Lord's promise. But on this day "two men returned. They came down from the hills and passed over and came to Joshua the son of Nun, and they told him all that had happened to them. And they said to Joshua, 'Truly the LORD has given all the land into our hands. And also, all the inhabitants of the land melt away because of us" (Joshua 2:23–24). They were a generation ready to possess their divine inheritance.

With this news in hand, Joshua began directing the people to prepare themselves for the great things that were about to happen. He told the people to keep their eyes upon the ark of the covenant, that they "may know the way you shall go, for you have not passed this way before" (Joshua 3:4). He then told the people "Consecrate yourselves, for tomorrow the LORD will do wonders among you" (Joshua 3:5). The next day he told them that the sign the Lord was going to give to them, as proof of His presence, would come when the feet of the priests bearing the ark touched the waters of Jordan: the waters would part and leave a path on the dry ground for them to cross (Joshua 3:7–13). Just as promised, the waters parted and a path was supplied.

Once the people had crossed over to the other side, the Lord told Joshua to take one man from each tribe, carry a rock from the river in the place where the priests stood, and put the rocks in the place where they spent the first night in the Promised Land. Why would they be told to gather rocks from the river? The rocks were to be set up as a memorial commemorating the power of God among His people. Joshua told the people, "When your children ask their fathers in times to come, 'What do these stones mean?' then you shall let your children know, 'Israel passed over this Jordan on dry ground.' For the LORD your God dried up the waters of the Jordan for you until you passed over, as the LORD your God did to the Red Sea, which he dried up for us until we passed over, so that all the peoples of the earth may know that the hand of the LORD is mighty, that you may fear the LORD your God forever" (Joshua 4:21-24). What do these stones mean? God is ever powerful and present among His people.

Before we point fingers at the children of Israel who failed to cross the Jordan the first time because of doubt, we modern "believers" may need to look in a mirror to see how similar we are to them. The children of Israel were brought out of Egyptian bondage through many miracles, including the blood of a Passover lamb that was sacrificed on their behalf. We were brought out of our own spiritual bondage through the miraculous death of the Lamb of God, who was slain on our behalf. Unlike the Passover lamb, our Lamb was raised from the dead three days later and is now seated at God's right hand. The children of Israel experienced many miracles on their way to possess the land of promise. We too have experienced miracles in our walks with the Lord. But when faced with adversity, we are like the children of Israel in that we forget all the former victories in the Lord. We can see only the impending defeat the enemy will hand us. We run into the wilderness and eventually die off.

Rather than be like the first generation of Israelites, we need to become more like the second generation. We need to remember the former victories and miraculous provisions of the Lord in previous situations. We need to set up stones of memorial that commemorate those past miracles of provision and deliverance. Then, when we or our children face adversity, we can look at the stones of memorial, smile, and declare that He will see us through.

Spiritual Pep Talks

In 1980, a brash young group of hockey players fresh from the college ranks found themselves facing the mighty veteran Russian hockey team. Having won gold in every Olympics since 1960, the Russian team made a formidable foe. In their first meeting just days before the opening ceremonies in Lake Placid, the young team from the USA was ravaged by the Soviets in Madison Square Garden by a score of 10 to 3. Coach Herb Brooks knew his team was in trouble that night as they stood in awe of the mighty Russians, applauding them as they came out on the ice.

During the week the followed, the attitude of the young team changed and their confidence was growing. The day before the game, goalie Jim Craig said to Coach Brooks, "Coach, you just wait. You haven't seen it yet."[3] Minutes before the opening face-off, Coach Brooks entered the locker room and "delivered a Knute Rockne-like message: 'You are born to be a player,' he said, reading from notes he had scribbled. 'You are meant to be here at this time. This is your moment.'"[4] In the remaining ten seconds of the contest, Al Michaels proclaimed the now famous line "Do you believe in miracles?" as the young lads from the USA defeated the old veteran ice warriors from Russia by a score of 4-3. A properly delivered pep talk stirred the young team, giving them the confidence they needed to defeat the adversary.

1 Samuel 17 finds the children of Israel facing an old familiar foe, the Philistines. This time, however, the Philistines came with a special weapon: a giant of a man named Goliath. As the two armies gathered in battle array on either side of the Valley of Elah, the Philistine champion came to the middle of the battleground and issued a challenge to the armies of Israel.

> "Why have you come out to draw up for battle?
> Am I not a Philistine, and are you not servants of
> Saul? Choose a man for yourselves, and let him
> come down to me. If he is able to fight with me
> and kill me, then we will be your servants. But if
> I prevail against him and kill him, then you shall
> be our servants and serve us." And the Philistine
> said, "I defy the ranks of Israel this day. Give me
> a man, that we may fight together." When Saul
> and all Israel heard these words of the Philistine,
> they were dismayed and greatly afraid (8–11).

Twice a day, for forty consecutive days, Goliath would approach the armies of Israel with his challenge. Every day for forty days, the men of Israel shook like trees in the wind. Even King Saul, who stood head and shoulders above the others, feared Goliath. As the king, Saul should have answered the challenge for the glory of Israel, but he instead offered a lucrative prize to any man who could kill Goliath.

Following the orders of his father, David appeared on the scene of the battle, only to bring provisions to his brothers and to return news of their well-being back to his father. When David was at the battleground, Goliath stepped forward to repeat his daily challenge. While all of the men of Israel fled from him, David wanted to know who he was and why he was allowed to defy the armies of the living God. David's courage riled his brothers but touched the heart of the king.

David was brought before the king, and he said to Saul, "Let no man's heart fail because of him. Your servant will go and fight with this Philistine." Imagine what went through Saul's mind when he realized his confident warrior was nothing but a boy. Saul tried to talk David out of certain death, but David walked in divine confidence as he said:

> "Your servant used to keep sheep for his father. And when there came a lion, or a bear, and took a lamb from the flock, I went after him and struck him and delivered it out of his mouth. And if he arose against me, I caught him by his beard and struck him and killed him. Your servant has struck down both lions and bears, and this uncircumcised Philistine shall be like one of them, for he has defied the armies of the living God." And David said, "The LORD who delivered me from the paw of the lion and from the paw of the bear will deliver me from the hand of this Philistine." (34–37)

Seeing that David could not be talked down, Saul offered David the king's armor. David tried the armor but rejected it, because he had no confidence in it. David had confidence in the weapons of a shepherd. So he took his staff, chose five stones from the brook, and with his sling in hand approached the Philistine.

When Goliath saw David coming at him with sticks and stones, he must have let out a laugh that shook the valley. Goliath asked, "Am I a dog, that you come to me with sticks? Come to me, and I will give your flesh to the birds of the air and to the beasts of the field" (43–44).

As David drew closer to the giant, his faith grew. He looked at the giant and said,

> You come to me with a sword and with a spear and with a javelin, but I come to you in the name of the LORD of hosts, the God of the armies of Israel, whom you have defied. This day the LORD will deliver you into my hand, and I will strike you down and cut off your head. And I will give the dead bodies of the host of the Philistines this day to the birds of the air and to the wild beasts of the earth, that all the earth may know that there is a God in Israel, and that all this assembly may know that the LORD saves not with sword and spear. For the battle is the LORD's, and he will give you into our hand. (45–47)

With that declaration, David rushed toward his enemy and hurled a single stone into Goliath's forehead, killing him. David then took the sword of Goliath and severed his head as a symbol of victory.

When the young shepherd David found himself facing the veteran champion Goliath, he could have easily focused on the size and experience of the adversary. Instead, David focused upon his own experiences of defeating both lions and bears that had tried to steal his sheep. David knew his victory was not in his own strength, but rather in the Lord who strengthened him. David gave himself a spiritual pep talk to remind himself how mighty God had been on his behalf. That pep talk gave him the confidence to go out against Goliath. He reminded himself that the battle belonged to the Lord and that the Lord Himself would supply the victory.

David was not the only saint who made use of a spiritual pep talk. In 2 Corinthians 1, Paul gives us his reasons for going through difficult times. In his first reason, Paul says that we go through adversity so that we learn to quit trusting in ourselves and to be fully dependent upon God. Paul stated that he had been through adversity so strenuous that he even despaired of life. But he was confident of this truth: if God delivered him then (past tense) and is delivering him now (present tense), then He will deliver him tomorrow (future tense). While not mentioning details in his letter, in his mind Paul replayed all of the times God had worked in his life— a personal spiritual pep talk.

Furthermore, Paul says that the second reason we go through difficult times is that we learn how to be comforted by God in the midst of our adversity. Once we have gone through our adversity, we meet others who are going through like circumstances, and we are able to comfort them in the way we were comforted. One way we do that is by giving a testimony of God's goodness toward us. That testimony can build up the faith of the listener, who in turn seeks God and is blessed—public spiritual pep talks.

Are you facing difficulties today? Are you in the middle of situations that seem hopeless? Before throwing in the towel, think back over your life and recall the times that God has blessed you in a miraculous way. Those events will help rekindle a faith within you that believes God will work in your behalf again.

Section II
Events before Knowing Christ

In this section I want to share a few stories of how God made His presence known in my life before I became a Christian. While I was raised by a Christian mother and went to church every Sunday, I had began casting off those restraints by the time I was fourteen years old. Each year I grew progressively worse until I turned twenty-one and all restraints were gone. Although I had kicked God out of my life, He remained active in spite of my rebellion. We may think by removing Him from our lives that He, or any thoughts of Him, will simply go away, but He remains forever present.

As a believer, it's easy to see where God is working in my life. After all, I bring my request before His throne and ask that He intervene in every situation of my life. When things begin to fall into place, such as the beginnings of this book, I can see how God is orchestrating every step. As a believer, I know that God is an ever-present help in time of need and that He is at work in me, bringing out His will in my life.

As a nonbeliever, that may be more difficult. As a nonbeliever, I am not in tune with a divine presence. I may "thank God" when something goes my way and ask him to curse something when things go awry, but in all reality those are only slang expressions that carry little or no significance. I will use terms like *luck, fate, coincidence,* and *karma* to explain why certain things occur. As a nonbeliever, I may not be aware of His presence, but He is there nonetheless.

It Came from the Closet

I remember when I was about twelve or thirteen, I shared a room with my brother, Mike. On several occasions I was awakened from a deep sleep by a voice clearly calling out my name. I would look at Mike to see what he wanted, but he would be sound asleep. I never told anyone about those nights. I was afraid they would think I was crazy.

When I got saved in 1987 and started reading my Bible again, I came across the story of Samuel. He was a "special" child conceived as a direct result of anguished prayer. His mother, Hannah, asked for a baby boy; if her request was granted, she would give the child back to God at weaning age. God answered her prayer and she kept her vow and gave the boy to Eli, the priest, to be raised in the temple. One night the boy heard a voice calling his name. He ran to Eli to see what he wanted. Each time Eli sent him away, saying that the boy was hearing things. On the third trip that night, Eli realized what was going on and told Samuel to respond to the voice with, "Speak Lord, for your servant is listening." That night Samuel became the prophet to the nation of Israel.

I was talking to my Grandpa Baker one day, and we got around to discussing this story. He looked at me with tears in his eyes and said that he, too, had heard his name called in the night, even as a grown man. His fear was that he had never responded to the voice and had missed a calling upon his life. He then told me that if I ever heard the voice again, I must answer the call.

I have never heard my name spoken in the night since those teenage years, but I know that I have heard the voice of God many times since. We can play down such events with comments like, "I was just hearing things," or, "I must have been dreaming." No matter what excuse we use to play it down, the fact remains that God is still calling people to salvation, to a deeper walk and into ministry. Has He called you by name? Have you heard His voice? Have you responded to the call?

The Tractor in the Ditch

When I was twelve years old, my brother and I worked in the hayfields for a man named Abner Bruce. We drove the mowing machines and rakes while Abner mowed and ran the baler. Once the hay was baled, Abner drove while Mike and I stacked the hay on the truck. We worked together unloading the hay in the barn. The next summer Mike got a job in town, and Abner's health prevented him from putting up his own hay, so he hired another crew to come and do the work, leaving me with nothing to do that summer. Abner hired me to brush-hog all of the fence lines in the hayfields after the baling was done and to clear some areas that were not good for hay but needed to be cleaned up for winter pasture.

One day I was mowing along a ditch that was several feet wide and about three feet deep. The sides of the ditch were steep, almost straight down. It would appear that to fall off the edge would result in a rollover. Remember, this was the early 1970s, and smaller tractors did not have cabs, roll cages, or seat belts. If you caused the tractor to roll over, you'd better hope you could jump away.

I had done well all morning working my way around the ditches, getting as close as I could, like Abner wanted. He had taught me to go slow in rough terrain, so I had the tractor in a low gear, creeping along. As I was working with a ditch to my left, the ground gave way and the tractor was heading into a rollover into the ditch. The next few seconds were a blur, but somehow I found my tractor sitting upright on the other side of the ditch, with me applying a death grip to the steering wheel. Needless to say, I was shaking like a leaf!

I shut the tractor down, got off, and checked the equipment for damage. Everything was fine. I then looked around to see if anyone was nearby. I was scared Abner saw what happened and was going to be mad at me. Then I walked over to the ditch and shook my head. The tractor had fallen off a sheer three-foot drop, turned at a left angle, hit the other side of the three-foot-high wall, come up at an angle, jumped out of the ditch, and landed four feet away.

That was thirty-one years ago and I am still amazed at what happened and what did not happen. That tractor should have rolled onto its side or nose-dived into the embankment on the other side, leaving it wedged in the ditch. When it didn't roll to the left, it should have rolled to the right when it hit the other side. It should never have come out of the ditch and landed upright, with no damage.

People might say this is a tall tale made up by a kid with a huge imagination. Others would say that the ditch was not really that deep, it only seemed that way to a kid. Of those who believe the story, many would call it luck. But some of us, I being the first, believe that God or His angels took over and brought me out safely. I never told Abner or my parents about this. In fact, I kept it quiet for a long time, for fear I would get into trouble.

Although I didn't become a believer for another fourteen years, I always believed that someone was looking out for me.

Ice Road Driving!

When I was about twenty years old, I was bold behind a steering wheel. I learned to drive on a farm under adverse conditions and was not afraid to drive on ice and snow. I had wrecked one truck on the ice, and from that day on, I learned what to do and what not to do.

I was still single and living at home, and we had bad weather move in that covered the roads for several days. While I had driven back and forth to work every day, I had not gone into town to see my friends for quite some time. It was Friday night and I was getting anxious to go to town and play. So I got into my four-wheel drive truck and headed out.

When I said I had learned from a previous accident what not to do, that means that even though I had a four-wheel drive truck, I could not fly down the highway like a normal day. I had to go slow and steady and pay attention. I was also taught to drive way out ahead of myself, looking for possible problems. About three miles north of town, there is a long sweeping curve on Route 66. As I looked around the curve, I noticed a car coming toward me at a high rate of speed—too fast for these conditions. I knew that if he couldn't turn the car on the curve, he would be sliding into my lane. I slowed down and, sure enough, he came sliding right for me. All I could do was ease onto the shoulder and eventually into the grass to keep from getting hit. After several rough and bumpy feet, I finally got the truck back up the shoulder and onto the road headed into town.

On my way home that night, I stopped to see the place where I'd slipped off the road. The grass off the shoulder was a steep slope down for several feet. There was a grass driveway that caused the bumps. This was a place that could have easily caused a truck to roll or slide sideways into the trees at the bottom. As I said, I came through the rough stuff, back onto the road, and went safely into town.

While I credit some of the outcome to my experience, I told my friends that night and again later that someone was watching over me. Whoever was watching kept me safe from harm. Even though I wasn't a Christian, I knew what had happened and who had kept me safe.

Gymnastics in Montana—
Perfect Ten!

In 1981 I was hired as a truck driver on a wheat harvest crew that traveled from Oklahoma through Kansas and Colorado, and finally into Montana. My job was simple. Each morning I either washed the windows of the combines or fueled them up. Once the combines were running, I chased them through the fields, catching the grain into the back of my truck. Once the truck was full, I would tarp the load down and head to the grain elevator. Once the truck was empty, I headed back to the field for more. It was a simple routine all day long, for as many trips as I could get in.

Sometimes when I returned to the field, I would have to check my grain bed, making sure the tarp bows and support chains were in place. Occasionally I would have to get into the bed and reset things. The top rail of the grain bed is only about two or three inches wide, just about like a gymnast's balance beam. After making this inspection several times a day, seven days a week, for four months, I was pretty good at walking that narrow rail from one end of the truck to the other, in cowboy boots.

I had pulled into a field in Montana and climbed up to do my routine inspection. Due to the rough roads into the fields, my last tarp bow had bounced out of the stake pocket and had fallen into the bed. I climbed up and stepped onto the bed rail and took off down the twenty-two-foot bed as I had done so many times before. I failed to see that one single grain of wheat sitting on the rail toward the end of the bed. I hit that grain of wheat at full speed, my foot flew out from under me, and I flew feet-first off the back of the truck. Not only did I fall ten feet to the ground, but I flew several feet out from the truck, landing flat on my back! Thank God for summer fallow! I landed in the dirt that had been tilled just a few weeks before, which made for a soft landing.

In Montana the winter temperatures are so extreme that the freezing of the soil pushes large, hard rocks to the surface. When I finally got up on my feet, I looked down where my head had hit, leaving a mark in the dirt. Just a couple of inches away was the top of a large rock. A couple of inches to the left, and it would have been a broken neck or cracked skull. Luck? I don't think so. Even in my sinful state at that time in my life, I looked up and whispered, "Thank You for a soft, safe landing." I knew someone had softened the landing.

There is a bit of humor to this story, of course. When I got back in my truck I heard my boss's voice over the radio. He said, "That was pretty good. I'll give you a nine. If you try it again, I bet you'll score a perfect ten!" My response? "No, thank you!"

Ten Commandments

It was Easter Sunday in 1987 and I had just gotten home from having surgery where I spent a lot of time on the couch watching television. That night I was home alone, watching *The Ten Commandments*[5], starring Charleton Heston. This is still one of my favorites. It wasn't the Bible story that I loved, but rather the cinematography involved with the miracles of the exodus. That night was different. I wasn't a Christian nor had I any desire to become one, so the events of the evening struck me as odd.

Around seven o'clock that evening, the movie reached the point where Moses was being exiled into the wilderness to die. (Just a note: Moses was not exiled, but rather fled Egypt out of fear, for killing an Egyptian.) The movie reaches a point where Moses is just about to be crushed by his circumstances. The narrator speaks of holy men and prophets being sent to such a place for the purpose of being beaten down into a mass that only God can use. As I watched that scene, I found myself weeping, unexplainably. My dad came in and I hid my face, so he could not see me and wonder what was wrong. I told no one about that night for a long time. It was simply buried at the back of my mind.

Shortly after I was saved, I came across a cassette my mom had of that Easter Sunday service at her church. I listened to the service. The music, the prayers, and the preaching were typical, nothing special. But then came the altar service. I would usually turn the tape off at this point, but something said to leave it on. Right there on the tape I heard several people praying for me—*by name!* I put two and two together. The service started at six o'clock. The altar call occurred around seven-thirty. The scene in the movie occurred at the same time as the altar call. Seven miles from the altar, God was using a scene in a movie to show me that I was going through that purging process. There is no distance with God, for He is everywhere at all times!

I hid the event in my heart for some time, even to the point of burying it under my sinful desires. But the event had occurred nonetheless. When the time was right, God put all the pieces together to show me how He used a Hollywood production of a biblical story to speak to my heart. Has He spoken to you in such a manner? Have you been moved in your heart through some form of media, but you could not explain why? Have you ever considered the fact that God Himself was trying to reach out to you in love? Things to consider.

September 14, 1981

Certain dates mark significant events in history that were major turning points in the lives of people. On a national level in America, we have such dates as the bombing of Pearl Harbor, of which President Roosevelt said, "Yesterday, December 7th, 1941—a date which will live in infamy."[6] In regard to the terrorist attack on the World Trade Center on September 11, 2001, President George W. Bush said, "Time is passing. Yet, for the United States of America, there will be no forgetting September the 11th."[7] In regard to the Murrah Building bombing on April 19, 1995, Vice-President Cheney said, "The United States has known some times of sadness both before and after the Murrah building was attacked, yet that spring morning ten years ago is still deeply etched in our memories."[8] These are the events that change our lives forever. These are the events in which time stands still.

While those events were experienced on a worldwide level, many of us have experienced events in our personal lives that few people know about, outside of family and friends. These events have changed us forever. September 14, 1981, was my day. It has been over thirty-one years since the actual event. It seems like it was yesterday. It seems like it was so long ago. It was my day when time stood still.

I had spent the summer driving trucks on wheat harvest for Larry Fenton. We had just returned to western Kansas to begin the fall harvest. It was a beautiful, sunny, cold Kansas morning. We had spent the past couple of hours prepping a combine so we could go pick pinto beans. I was given the task of digging swollen wheat clods out of a fourteen-inch auger, when it was accidentally engaged. Because my entire right arm was inside the auger system, it was instantly wrapped up in the auger flighting. I have never before or since experienced the level of pain that I felt in that moment. Within seconds my eyesight went snow white, and I remember crying, "I'm not ready to die! Oh, God! I'm not ready to die!" The next hour and a half was a whirlwind of events that seemed to run together. While I remember many of the events, some are very blurry. During a phone conversation with the nurse who was the head of the emergency crew that took care of me, all of the pieces were put into place, and I fully understood what happened that day.

While I thought I knew everything there was to know about the accident, I discovered that I knew only bits and pieces. Some of the vital information was never shared with me, nor was it in the reports I was given to read. Last year I found the nurse who was on the ambulance crew, and we spoke on the phone for several hours. She helped me put all of the pieces of the story together so that I could better understand what I went through. The best way to share the events is to list each one in sequence.

The cleanout door I was trapped in was just above the height of my shoulder. Therefore, Larry grabbed me by my belt and held me up, trying to relieve the pressure. I was later told that other men offered to hold me up in order to give Larry a break, but he refused to let me go. He held me in that position for approximately forty minutes. I also heard that it took a couple of days for Larry's fingers to straighten out and quit hurting.

Shortly after the initial impact, I felt a hard stick in my left arm, and I pulled it back. The nurse grabbed my arm and said she had to get an IV into me, but I told her that the needle hurt. Imagine that—in the midst of the most excruciating pain I have ever felt in my right side, I was complaining about a little needle in my left arm.

The day before, I had exchanged some harsh words with the parts guy down at the Chevy dealership over a windshield wiper motor for my grain truck. Now he was standing within inches of my face, eye-to-eye, applying compresses to my shoulder in hopes of stopping the bleeding. Be careful who you get mad at—they might just pop in and help save your life.

We tried several tricks to get my arm out of the combine. The first trick they tried was to turn the auger backward with a wrench, hoping the reverse spiral action would push my arm back out. All we got out of that was a greater level of pain.

The next trick was to remove all the bolts holding the auger housing together. This should have allowed the shield to fall away from the combine, thus letting my arm fall free. Once the bolts were out, they couldn't get the thing to pry apart, even with two hundred pounds of pressure on a small jaws spreader.

Finally a local welder crawled into a tiny space in the top of the auger and began cutting the auger apart. After several minutes I was finally free, and I felt them laying me back onto the gurney. I remember looking down and seeing my best friend and coworker crawling under the combine to the other side. He told me later he just didn't want to see my arm. I do not blame him. I have never seen what it looked like either.

We then took a forty-minute ride in an ambulance to Garden City, Kansas. Several things occurred during that ride that stand out to me.

I asked how fast we were going. They looked at me like I was crazy. Here I was at death's door, and I wanted to know how fast we were going! The driver said we were doing ninety-two miles per hour. He then said to hang on because we were about to take the hard right turn in Scott City that would send us south into Garden City. It really hurt my arm when we turned that corner, as it caused me to lean onto my right shoulder.

During the ride the nurse asked me where I was from. I was such a jerk! I said, "From Bristow, Oklahoma. Like you know where that is or could even care less. You're trying to keep me talking so I won't go into shock." She leaned in real close and smiled as she asked, "Do the kids still turn around at the Frosty Freeze?" Only a Bristow kid would know that! Turns out she was from Bristow, too. Small world. Nine hours from home, and I meet someone from home in such a scene as this.

As the nurse retold these stories, I began to remember bits and pieces. The next two things she told me shook me to the core. Two things I had never heard in the thirty years following the accident.

First she said, "Steve, you bled out." When I acknowledged that I knew I'd lost a lot of blood, she interrupted me and explained that from the time she arrived at the scene and started her IV until we arrived at the hospital, I survived on whatever fluids she was putting into me. There were only traces of red in the fluids that were coming out of the wounds.

The next thing she said was, "Steve, you left my ambulance for a moment, but you came right back." I acknowledged that I probably drifted in and out of consciousness with such a blood loss, but she interrupted again and said, "No, Steve. You left. You were gone. You stopped living and we had to do CPR to get you back, along with some very intense prayer." No, I never saw a bright light at the end of the tunnel, nor did I hear a voice telling me it was time to go back because I had work to do, nor did I have an out of body experience. I just came back.

I remember being wheeled into the emergency room. It seemed big and bright. It still amazes me what little things I noticed. I was so exhausted that I just lay there. I remember feeling my clothes being cut off of me. I heard my boots hit the floor and the pliers I carried slide into a wall. I remember looking up into the sweetest set of eyes and telling her how tired I was. She told me that everything was okay and that I could go to sleep and rest. I remember waking up again and gagging on a tube running down my throat. I couldn't breathe and I panicked. To get one man's attention, I hit him in the ribs. He turned around and, I guess, put me back under.

The next thing I remember was waking up to the sound of a voice calling out loudly to someone named Ronnie. My first thought was, "Shut up, I'm trying to sleep over here!" I later learned that Ronnie was in a coma sustained from a car wreck he had been in, and they were trying to communicate with him as they were told. The pain in my right arm was unreal. I kept reaching for my right arm, trying to check the damage, but I could not find the arm. This added more confusion to the situation. How could something hurt so bad, yet not be touched? I then turned to the left and saw Larry and his friend standing there. I asked him about my arm. As tears welled up in the eyes of this huge, manly man, he lowered his head and turned away. I looked at his friend, and she told me the arm was gone.

Although thirty years have passed, that is the moment that is forever etched in my mind. That is the moment when time stood still.

When I think back to that day, I am deeply humbled to know the depths to which God's love and mercy will reach. When I consider my lifestyle at the time of the accident, God in His justice had every right to look at me and say that I was simply reaping the fruit of my lifestyle and then walk away and let me die. However, in His mercy He chose to stand in that trailer park, ride in that ambulance, and enter that emergency room, holding me and strengthening each one of those present. When I think of the countless other people who do not survive such events, it makes me ask why.

One Step Ahead

In 1987 I suffered the loss of many things. By the time the year was over, I had lost everything. I have often said that if my parents had not let me live at home for free, I would have been homeless or dead. In the first four months of that year, I had reached a point of deep depression. I had honestly gotten to the point where I wanted to call it quits. I was finished. It was time to put an end to it all.

I had just finished taking one of my daily walks. Instead of going back inside, I sat down in the grass at the end of the house. I mulled over what my life had become, and I wasn't pleased. As I sat there, I started thinking about getting my gun, heading off to the woods, and pulling the trigger. As I got up to go into the house, my neighbor pulled into the drive. My first thought was, "Why are you home this time of day, and why are you pulling into my drive to bother me? I've got things to do." Instead, I was nice and waited for him to get out of his truck. The first thing he did was ask if I was okay. I told him I was fine. *Liar.* He then said, "Well, I was at work and I couldn't shake the feeling that something was wrong. So I told my boss that I needed to get here and check on you. I hurried as fast as I could. Glad to see you're okay. Bye, now." And he drove away.

As he drove away I stood there thinking about what he'd said. He said he felt like something was wrong, and he needed to get home and see me. He worked forty-five minutes away. How did he know something was wrong and forty-five minutes later pull into my drive at just the right moment? Although I was not a Christian at the time of that event, and did not become a believer for a couple more months, I looked up into the heavens that day and thought, "How did You do that?" I never contemplated suicide again.

A few years later I went to preach in my home church. My subject that day was listening to the promptings of the Spirit, no matter how crazy they may seem, and following through. It was one of those sermons that needed a good life lesson. As I walked off the stage and down the center aisle, I told them this story. I made it as generic as possible. Then I stood in front of my friend and said, "That was you and me. Remember? That day, your obedience stopped a suicide. Thank you." He'd had no clue until that moment.

I can only pray that my spirit is so in tune with God's Spirit that He can communicate with me the way He did with my neighbor. Maybe He can use me to help guide another person through a dark and perilous time. When they are not willing to listen or are unable to hear the voice of the Father for themselves, I pray that I can hear God for them and be His hands, His feet, His eyes, His ears, and His mouth.

Section III
Events after Knowing Christ

In this section, I want to share a few stories of how God made His presence known in my life after I became a Christian. As a believer, it is easy to see where God is working in my life. I bring my requests before His throne and ask that He intervene in every situation of my life. When things begin to fall into place, such as the beginnings of this book, I can see how God is orchestrating every step. As a believer, I know that God is an ever-present help in time of need and that He is at work in me, bringing out His will in my life.

You Are Who You Said You Are!

I remember the night I prayed what turned out to be a very dangerous prayer. After losing my right arm, having surgery on my left shoulder, and all the "stuff" that was going on in my life in 1987, sleep was very hard to come by. Not only did I toss and turn a lot, but when I did sleep, I snored like a freight train. My tossing and turning kept me awake, and my snoring kept my folks awake. Oftentimes they would shut my door to block the noise.

That afternoon I had read a little article in a devotional periodical called *Guideposts*. The article was about a woman who desperately needed help and was not sure whether she could really trust this man called Jesus that everyone was telling her about. So she prayed, "If you are who you say you are, could you show me?" The gist of her article was that He did indeed prove Himself to her in a miraculous way.

My usual custom was to go to bed and pray until I fell asleep. That night I got into bed, lay flat on my back, pulled the covers up to my chin, looked up to the dark ceiling, and said, "Jesus, if You are who You say You are, prove it to me." At that moment, it felt as if another blanket settled onto my bed, and that is all I remember.

I woke up the next morning between seven and eight. As I looked up at the ceiling, I realized that my covers had not been messed up, nor had I moved all night. I felt completely rested when my mom looked in and saw me awake. She asked whether I was okay. It seems I never made a sound all night. My parents were concerned because I was so quiet all night that they'd even checked to see if I was still breathing. After telling her I was okay, I looked to the heavens and quietly stated, "I can never doubt who You are again."

Although I have fallen along the way, strayed from the narrow path on occasion, and played the hypocrite all too often, there is one unshakable truth that I know: *He is who He says He is!*

Be Careful to Keep Your Vows

In the spring of 1989 I attended a night class that my pastor was teaching at a Bible college in Oklahoma City. While there on campus I realized that the time had come to go to college and learn how to be a better preacher. Being single, with little income, my plan was to live in the dorms starting in the fall of that year. I had one problem: I had no transportation and no money to buy a car.

I was visiting my grandparents one afternoon when my granddad began asking me questions. He asked, "So I hear you're planning on going to school in Oklahoma City in the fall?" I answered, "Yes, sir." He then asked, "How do you plan on getting there without a car?" I answered, "I figure I can ride a bus or someone can take me there and drop me off." He then said, "Might be kind of difficult without a car, that is, being afoot in a strange town and all." I answered, "Yes. But I can manage." He then held up a set of keys to his old, navy blue Dodge Reliant K and said, "I am buying myself a new car, and I want to give this one to you to go to school in." I was humbled, yet still filled with enough pride to say, "I appreciate that and I'll take you up on it. And I'll pay you back if I ever have enough money." He snatched the keys away and said, "I guess I'll find someone else who needs it more than you." At that point, I was fully humbled and accepted his gift.

As I drove away in my "new car," I praised the Lord for his supply without my telling anyone of my need or plans. I then became brash in my praise and declared, "Because you have given me transportation in this car, I will share my gift with others that have a like need." Down the road I went, forgetting the wise words of the preacher in Ecclesiastes 5:4–6: "When you vow a vow to God, do not delay paying it, for he has no pleasure in fools. Pay what you vow. It is better that you should not vow than that you should vow and not pay. Let not your mouth lead you into sin, and do not say before the messenger that it was a mistake. Why should God be angry at your voice and destroy the work of your hands?" I would remember those words a few days later.

I was on my way to town one evening to attend a home Bible study. As I turned onto Highway 66 headed toward town, I saw a man sitting on the side of the road with his legs crossed. As I got near, he held up a thumb like he wanted a ride. The first thought that went through my mind was, "If you have no more ambition than to sit there and hold up a thumb, I have no time for you," and I drove by. As I glanced in the rearview mirror, I saw him looking at me with his arms spread wide as if to say, "Why not? Is there a problem?" Then a voice echoed through my head, "You made a vow—a promise. And now you refuse to keep it?" I immediately stopped, backed up, and offered a ride.

As the man climbed into the car with his small bag, I naturally looked him over. His hair was long and matted. He looked as if he had not shaved for a couple of weeks. His ratty black T-shirt carried the emblem of a skull and crossbones.

He stank to high heaven! I turned away and prayed under my breath, "Okay, Lord. You're gonna have to help me here with this smell." When I looked back at the guy, I detected no odor. It was as if it had simply disappeared. He apologized for not getting up to hail a ride but said he really didn't feel well. He then thanked me for the ride, and we headed for town.

During the ride, he asked how far I was going. I told him I was going to town to attend a Bible study. He smiled and said that that was a good thing to do. I asked if he wanted to go with me, but he said he just wanted to get to someplace where he could rest. For some reason the thought never crossed my mind about asking the Ministerial Alliance for help. He insisted that I drop him off on the other side of town. I dropped him off at a little store and offered him a few bucks, which he reluctantly accepted. As I drove away, I watched him walk into the store.

I went to the Bible study and told everyone what had happened. My mentor asked whether I had called the alliance, and I said I had forgotten about them. When I heard a storm rolling in, I decided to head to the store to see if he was around and get him some help if he was. When I went into the store, I asked if they remembered him. They said they saw me pull up, sit for a few minutes, and then drive away; they even wondered if I was okay. I was honestly concerned for his well-being, but he was gone.

I stopped at my regular store to get something and talk to a friend before heading home. While standing there, a little old man I knew from around town was complaining that he needed to get home but was afraid he was going to get wet before he got there because he had no car. I offered a ride, but he humbly refused. When we saw some lightning through the window, I offered again, and he played it down again, making it sound

Steve Wheeler

like it was out of my way. I told him this was his last chance, and I headed to the car. Just as I started the engine, a loud clap of thunder shook the place. He came running out, jumped in the car, and said, "Okay, kid! I'll take you up on it!"

On my way home and later in my room, I thought about those two men. While I could account for the little old man in town, I could not account for the hitchhiker. I thought about how guilty I felt when I refused to give him a ride. I thought about the way the smell disappeared, his pleasant demeanor and warm smile. I thought about how he just disappeared. I thought about the voice reminding me of my vow from a few days before. I had to ask myself, "Did I just entertain an angel and not realize it?" I don't know about the angel, but I know I was tested that night.

For the Love of Ripley

There is a small country church in the small town of Ripley, Oklahoma, in which I have preached numerous times over the years. I preached my first Mother's Day and Father's Day sermons in this church when my friend Mark Wilson was the pastor. I have also served as interim pastor on two occasions. Needless to say, this church holds a special place in my heart. But the main reason it does is the miracle that was performed in my dad's life on a particular Sunday morning there.

Before I became a Christian, my dad and I would spend Sunday nights together watching television and eating dinner. We were very close at that point in my life. Once I became a Christian, I started going to church on Sunday mornings and evenings. Each Sunday, especially Sunday evening, I would ask my dad if he would like to go to church with me. Our conversation would be the same every week. I would ask, "Would you like to go to church with me?" Without looking in my direction he would say, "No." I would smile and say, "I have to ask." He would reply, "I have to say no."

I noticed one week that my dad refused to speak to me. It was as if he were avoiding me. I asked him if he was mad, and he said everything was fine, but that is where the conversation ended. So I asked my mother whether she knew what the problem was. Her answer shocked me. She said he was upset with me because I did not invite him to church with me. It turned out that on a particular Sunday night when I was going to preach, I was so caught up with my message that I walked out the door without asking my dad whether he wanted to go to church with me. The following Sunday I remembered to ask my question, "Would you like to go to church with me?" Without looking in my direction he said, "No." I smiled and said, "I have to ask." He replied, "I have to say no." That was our Sunday routine until the day I moved away from Bristow.

A couple of years later I was visiting with my dad, and out of the blue he said, "I would like to hear you preach sometime. I won't go to that church in town, but if you get a chance to preach at Ripley or Welty [another country church near Bristow], I will go with you."

Okay. Several weeks later I was getting dressed for church on a Sunday morning when the phone rang. It was Pastor Mark from Ripley. He told me that he had to go out of town and needed me to fill the pulpit for him. Naturally, I said yes. Then my dad's words crossed my mind: "I would like to hear you preach sometime. I won't go to that church in town, but if you get a chance to preach at Ripley or Welty, I will go with you." Later that day I called dad and told him that I was going to preach in Ripley. He said, "And I made you a promise that I would go and listen, and I will keep that promise."

The Sunday came for our trip to Ripley. Mom was out of town, so it was just the two of us. When we pulled up to the church, he said, "Point me to the nearest coffee shop, and tell me what time church starts. I want to come in late and sit in the back row. And if anyone introduces me or points me out, I'm going to get up and leave." Right before church started I went up and told the chairman of the service, the music leader, and the choir, "There will be a dark-headed man in a flannel shirt and blue corduroys coming in late. That is my dad. If he gets identified publicly in any way, he will leave." Everyone understood and, sure enough, he came in about ten minutes into the service.

After the service was over, I stood at the back door and greeted all the people. I figured Dad would go on out to the car, but he stood there by me. After shaking my hand, people would smile at him and shake his hand as if they had known him forever. Finally, a man named Red came by. After shaking my hand, he introduced himself to my dad. He said, "My name's Red and it is really great to have you here this morning." Dad replied, "I'm Cletis Wheeler from Bristow." Red replied, "Wheeler from Bristow? Interesting. Our preacher is a Wheeler from Bristow. Do you know each other?" My dad put his arm on my shoulder and said, "This is my son." What I haven't told you yet is that my dad had disowned me for a couple of years. He publicly denied to several people that I was his son.

On the drive home my dad started asking why all of those people were so friendly to him after church. They did not know him, so he could not understand why they treated him so nicely. He said it made him feel good, the way they reached out to him. I told him, "Dad, they reached out to you because they love you." He said, "But they don't know me." I said, "I know. They don't have to know you. The love that God has placed in their hearts causes them to reach out to strangers. And that feeling you're talking about is the love." He talked about that all the way home. In a small country church in the middle of Oklahoma, my dad experienced the love of God firsthand.

Shortly after Dad's death, I returned to Ripley. Before starting my message, I told them I had something to share. I said,

"You all have been used and you don't even know it." Before I continued, Brother Ben Craig blurted out in a frustrated tone, "What did we do now?" I continued, "Hold on, Brother, let me finish. You were used by the Lord, as a group, to demonstrate His love to a man who had never experienced it." I went on to share the story of Dad's visit to the church, his later salvation experience, and finally his death. You could see the emotions of joy sweep over the crowd. Brother Ben asked, "We did that? Well, *praise the Lord!*"

The first lesson we can learn from this experience is that God often uses those that seem to be insignificant or hidden in obscurity. Ripley is a small country church located in a tiny rural town in the middle of central Oklahoma. But the people in the fellowship were available to be a channel for God's love to a stranger. You may feel like an insignificant person hidden from the rest of the world, but you can still touch lives without realizing it. In Acts 9:10–19, the Lord sent a man named Ananias to pray for a man named Saul. While Ananias slips in and out of biblical history in a few short verses, Saul becomes Paul, writes the majority of the New Testament, and turns the world upside down for Jesus.

The second lesson we can learn from this experience is for the church. All too often visitors come to our churches and have to sit toward the front, where they are on display. We watch them during the service to see how they act. We might even whisper to our neighbor, asking about the visitors. When church is over, we are either so caught up in getting out the door or connecting with our best friend that we fail to greet the visitors. We never make them feel welcome. We never demonstrate the love of God.

Dad's Salvation

Following my accident in 1981, my dad and I were forced to spend a lot of time together. He was with me during my three-week stay in a Kansas hospital; and when we returned to Oklahoma, he drove me to therapy three days a week and changed my bandages throughout the day. As I healed we continued to do the chores necessary for running the farm. From that experience we grew close. It was the type of closeness that included never needing to speak when doing chores, because we knew what the other was thinking.

In early 1988 my dad went through a major ordeal involving substance abuse, much like I had the year before. While I got clean through my salvation experience, my dad had to do a stint in a rehab center. During a group session I was grilled about my former lifestyle, and I was asked how I was set free. I told them that my deliverance from my problems came as a direct result of my becoming a Christian. I also told them that Jesus could do the same for every one of them. This seemed to irritate the group leader, who had started the grilling process. Although he'd asked, he did not like my answers. He immediately ended the session.

Back in Dad's room, a volunteer named Tom came in. Dad asked Tom, "Do you have to get saved in order to get clean and leave this place?" Tom looked at me, which told me news had already traveled throughout the wing. He looked back at Dad and said, "No, you don't, but I want to show you something." He came back into the room with two books. One was very thick, while the other was very thin. He said, "This thick book is filled with people who have passed through the clinic without accepting Jesus. The book is thick because they keep coming back. The thin book, on the other hand, is filled with people who have been through the clinic, made peace with Jesus, and never returned. Mr. Wheeler, I'm in the thin book." At that moment, my dad looked away from me and shunned me for the next two years.

During that two-year period, I would call home, and if Dad answered and heard my voice, he would hand the phone to Mother. If I came in one door, he would go out the other. If we were forced to sit at the same table, he would turn to one side or the other, covering his vision with one hand so he could not see me. The hardest thing I experienced occurred one day when he was talking about his children, Mike and Cleta. Someone said, "What about Steve?" He said, "I don't know who you're talking about." I was disowned over knowing Jesus.

I continued to pray for my dad. I would send him notes telling him that I missed him and loved him very much. He would read the card and ask my mother what I meant. She would say, "Simple. He loves you and he misses you."

Over the next few years, I developed a deep burden for my dad. Even though I prayed for him daily, nothing seemed to happen. Then I was shown two new ways to pray for him, and things began to change.

The first way I prayed for my dad was based upon a story I heard. The mom stated that she used to pray for her lost son using a momma's sentimental heart: "Lord, he's a good kid and just needs a change in direction. Please save my son." No change ever came in the boy's life. She then began to pray, not for the boy as her son, but as a person, "Lord, [name] is lost. If he dies tonight, he goes to hell. That is not Your will, because You do not desire the death of the wicked. I pray that Your will would be done in the life of [name], and he would come to a saving knowledge in Jesus Christ." The young man came to Christ in a short time! I began praying the same prayer, putting my dad's name in the blank. I no longer prayed for "my dad" but began praying for the man, Cletis Wheeler.

The second way I prayed was to claim a promise found in Malachi 4:6: "And he will turn the hearts of fathers to their children and the hearts of children to their fathers, lest I come and strike the land with a decree of utter destruction." I knew God would restore our relationship. When I was thirty-one years old, I heard my dad say for the first time, "I'm proud of you." When I was thirty-five, I heard him say for the first time, "I love you."

In 1995 we came to visit the family. Due to his throat cancer, he was forced to wear a trachea tube. He was not allowed to eat, but rather put everything through a feeding tube. One night he put a piece of hard candy in his mouth just for taste. The thick syrup got stuck in his throat, and he began to choke. Mom finally got him suctioned out and breathing again. As I sat on the coffee table watching this, he looked at me and said, "I'm ready to meet your God." I told him, "I'm not going to talk to you like a son, but as a preacher. I need to know. You are either ready to meet Him as your savior or die and meet Him as your judge." He said, "You are right on both accounts." After a few more words, I led him in praying the

Sinner's Prayer. That night the son who was disowned as the preacher was given the awesome privilege of leading his dad into the presence of the Lord.

While his health never came back, his spirit grew sweeter every day. He was not bitter about life or what it had dealt him. Because he could no longer speak, I typed up a detailed testimony of the events of that night. He kept that paper on the coffee table and insisted that it be read by everyone who came to visit. He died in October of that year. Per his request, I preached his funeral.

Following Christ can come with a heavy price. In my case, I lost my dad and friend for a while. But we must remain faithful to the Lord and love and pray for those who hate us. One day God will restore those relationships, and he may even give you the opportunity to lead your loved one to His throne.

Section IV
The Living Word

In this section, I want to share a few stories of how God used his written Word to reveal Himself to me and make His presence known in my life. While the first story occurred before I became a believer, I include it in this section because it demonstrates the power God's Word can have upon our lives. That single event was a major turning point in my life in that it helped bring me back to the Lord. The remaining stories occurred after I became a believer. The stories demonstrate times when the Word was used to give clear directions in how to handle various situations.

As a believer, I read my Bible every day. Second Timothy 3:16–17 states, "All Scripture is breathed out by God and profitable for teaching, for reproof, for correction, and for training in righteousness, that the man of God may be complete, equipped for every good work." By reading the Bible daily, we learn what the will of God is for our lives and the world in which we live. We learn how to live in such a way as to bring honor to God. The Word of God becomes the bread that helps our inner man grow stronger each day.

I have also discovered, as many other believers have, that the Word of God is more than the mere words written upon the page. Hebrews 4:12 states, "For the word of God is living and active, sharper than any two-edged sword, piercing to the division of soul and of spirit, of joints and of marrow, and discerning the thoughts and intentions of the heart." It has often been said that people read the same verses over and over and see the surface teaching only. Then, one day while reading the same passage, the words seem to jump off the page and speak directly to the reader's heart. It is in those times that the Spirit of God illuminates a certain passage of Scripture, giving the reader clear and precise direction for what he or she is facing in life.

Judged!

In 1986 I had gotten back together with a young woman that I had dated off and on over the past ten years. While I cannot speak for her, I know at that time in my life I loved this young woman deeply. At ages twenty-six and twenty-two, we wanted to spend time together as most adult couples that are in love do. We wanted to be intimate. The only problem was that we were not in the financial position of getting married and living on our own. At the time, I was out of work and trying to go back to school, so I was stuck with either living at home or in the dorm. She was still stuck at her parents' house. It was a tough situation.

While I was in school, we found creative ways to be together. We would meet either in the town where she worked or in the town where I went to school and sleep at an area motel. To pull this off, we had to tell lies to all parties involved. While I lived in the dorms, I would check out and tell the Resident Parent that I was heading back to my home town for the night and would be back the next day. Hopefully, if my parents called, no one would figure things out; they'd leave a message and I would call them when I came in. My story would be that I was out with a few friends, and it was late when I got in. My friend would tell her parents that she was staying with a friend and would be home the next day. This worked well for several months.

In January of 1987 I began having trouble with my arm. I found myself either dropping things that I should not drop or waking up in the night with my arm too numb to move. After going to the doctor and having things checked out, the diagnosis was thoracic outlet syndrome. This occurs when the arteries and nerves running to the arm become pinched between the top rib and the collarbone. Turns out, I was slowly killing off my only arm. The procedure used to correct the problem was known as a rib resection. In this surgery, they would go in by the collarbone and remove the top rib and any muscle tissue that was squeezing on the arteries and nerves, thus relieving the pressure. The procedure was a success, but I had to quit school for a while and thus lost any alibis or ways of getting together with my friend.

After several weeks of not being together, my friend and I decided that we needed to be alone for the night. We decided to meet at a motel in Tulsa just a few blocks from where she worked. While she had an alibi, I did not. It was hard to do, but I went against everything I had been taught, even by a father who had no religious beliefs but was a moral person. I went up to my Christian mother, looked her in the eye, and said, "I am going to Tulsa to spend the night with my friend. I'll be back tomorrow morning." I could tell by the look in her eye that she was hurt and angry all at once. She never raised her voice but quietly said, "Your unsaved father would not even do something like this." While I did not understand her remark until later in life, I simply said, "I'm not my father." I got in my truck and drove away.

Never tell your Christian mother that you are going to spend the night in a motel with your girlfriend. A good Christian mother never screams or rants at you; she simply prays for you. She gets alone with God and talks to Him about you. She tells Him how bad you are and how you are doing harmful things. She agrees with Him that a soul bent on living like this deserves hell, but she also reminds Him that He takes no delight in the death of the wicked but desires that all men come to a knowledge of the truth. She reminds God that His Son, Jesus, came to seek and to save sinners, and that her son needed saving.

It takes forty-five minutes to drive from my mother's house to the motel in Tulsa. I pulled up to the motel, checked in, got the key, and found the room. My friend pulled up just as I was walking up to the door. We unlocked the door and turned on the light, and she went in first. Just as we stepped in the door, there was a writing table to the left, and on the table was a Bible. That Bible was left open. She looked down at the pages, pointed to a place on the page, laughed, and said, "I don't believe that." I looked down where she had pointed and read the words, and for a moment, my blood ran cold and my heart shuddered. But I closed the Bible, put my bag on top of the book as if to hide it from view, and went about our sinful evening.

About four o'clock in the morning, I woke up. I looked around the dimly lit room. I saw my friend sleeping next to me. I looked over and saw my bag sitting on the desk. I remembered what was under the bag. As I lay there looking at my friend and my surroundings, I softly whispered, "What in the world am I doing here?" Within the next hour, we were both up and getting dressed, because she had to be at work by six-thirty. We gathered our stuff, and once again, I saw the Bible lying there.

We stepped outside and were saying our good-byes, with plans for that evening. She looked at me and asked if I was all right. Naturally, I said I was fine. She shook her head no and said, "Something is wrong. I can tell by your eyes. Your eyes look worried, even scared. What's wrong?" After a few minutes of urging, I convinced her I was fine, and she drove away.

I got in my truck and sat there for a few minutes. I was not okay. I was scared. I was worried. I was a nervous wreck. You see, within the forty-five minutes it took to drive from my mother's presence to that motel, God had moved in her behalf. He prepared a room, a table, and an open Bible to bring me to a knowledge of His truth, as painful as it may be. That night the Bible was not left open to a passage of Scripture talking about love, or mercy, or grace. It was a verse about divine judgment. The words on the page my friend laughed at made my blood run cold: "Let marriage be held in honor among all, and let the marriage bed be undefiled, for God will judge the sexually immoral and adulterous" (Hebrews 13:4). That night I stood in judgment. The next few weeks were a whirlwind of confusion and bad decisions. I did things that drove my friend away. I was all alone and standing in judgment. Little did I know at that time, God was in the process of bringing my sinful world to an end, to walk me into the glorious life He had prepared for me. I later learned that God's judgment is not for the purpose of destruction; rather, it is redemptive in its nature, as it brings us to the end of ourselves, causing us to cry out to Him. And when we cry out, He answers.

One thing to learn from this experience is that God still judges sin. He still holds people accountable for their actions. The beautiful thing is, however, He will not let them go into eternity lost, without giving them every opportunity to see the light. Remember, God takes no delight in the death of the wicked, but rather that they should turn from their ways and live (Ezekiel 18:23). He desires that all men come to a knowledge of His truth and the gift of eternal life, and He will go to great lengths to reach that person.

A second thing we can learn from this experience is that when a lost love is at his or her worst, God is at His best. When that person is determined to go to the pigpens of life, God will meet them there. He will wait for them with patient arms. Pray for them. Pray His will over them. Trust Him. He can do amazing things when we let Him.

A New Thing

Since becoming a Christian in 1987, waking up at two o'clock in the morning has become a common occurrence. When I suddenly wake up from a sound sleep and see two o'clock on the radio, I know to say, "I'm here Lord and I'm listening." Some nights everything remains silent, and I know to simply offer praise until I go back to sleep. Other nights, He floods my mind with passages of Scripture and thoughts about His kingdom.

This practice started on June 7, 1988, when I was shaken from a sound sleep. Instantly my mind was filled with the text of Isaiah 43. At first I was reluctant, because I wanted to sleep. However, the verse refused to go away. I got my Bible and began reading. My eyes then locked on a particular verse that reads, "Behold, I will do a new thing; now it shall spring forth; shall ye not know it? I will even make a way in the wilderness, and rivers in the desert" (Isaiah 43:19 KJV). Over the next few days, I pondered that verse and felt bad that I did not seem to understand.

On the night of July 7, once again I was shaken from a sound sleep. This time my mind was filled with the name Habakkuk. Habakkuk? At two in the morning? I hate to admit it, but I had to look in my table of contents to find this obscure little prophet. Once there, however, I discovered that his words are neither obscure nor little. In fact, they carried quite a punch as I read, "Behold ye among the heathen, and regard, and wonder marvellously: for I will work a work in your days, which ye will not believe, though it be told you" (Habakkuk 1:5 KJV). What a rebuke! The Lord was telling me that He was going to do something in my life, something that I refused to believe, even though I had been told!

The next morning I prayed over the words and apologized to the Lord for my stubborn heart that seemed so hard to penetrate. I decided to listen to a tape of a sermon by a preacher named Ben Jordan. His text was taken from Leviticus 6:13, which states, "The fire shall ever be burning upon the altar; it shall never go out." He went on to tell several stories about how the fire of God had landed in the hearts of certain people throughout history. His key line in each story was, "In that quiet little scene, no one saw it, no one heard it, no one felt it, but fire landed in the heart of [name]." That morning I understood the two texts the Lord had shared with me. That morning, all alone in my parents' kitchen, no one saw it, no one heard it, no one felt it, but fired landed in my heart, and I was forever changed.

The next time you find yourself having one of those "I cannot sleep" kind of nights, or if you suddenly wake up and cannot go back to sleep, do not be so quick to jump on the computer or turn on the television. You probably will not find what you are looking for there, nor will you find the sleep you need. Grab your Bible, get on your knees, and say, "I am here, Lord. I am listening." You will be surprised at the wonderful things the Lord can share with you when your mind is quiet.

Do the Work of an Evangelist

One day in 1987 I was extremely antsy. I could not sit still for anything. There was nothing going on at the time to cause this, so I was at a loss. I roamed the house trying to find a place to rest until my appointment in Sapulpa later that day. Finding no place to rest, I took a walk and then messed around outside for a while. Nothing helped and rest was not to be found.

In desperation I went out to the couch in the living room, buried my head in the cushions, and began crying out to God. I prayed for peace, but peace never came. I began asking what was missing, what I needed to do—*what are You telling me*? In my mind, I began hearing a verse of Scripture: 2 Timothy 4. Naturally, I grabbed my Bible and began reading. Then my eyes fell on verse 4, "As for you, always be sober-minded, endure suffering, do the work of an evangelist, fulfill your ministry." As I pondered that verse and accepted the truth it revealed to me, peace flooded my soul and the antsy-ness disappeared.

There are times in our lives when we cannot rest. We go through every means possible to find the rest we crave, but it eludes us. I believe it eludes us because God creates a restlessness in us, which causes us to run to Him. Once in His presence, we hear His voice and His words for us, and then peace comes to our hearts.

The Prayer by the Pond

In March of 1988 I found myself being torn in two on the issue of being a preacher. On the one hand, I had some people telling me that they just knew that I had been called to preach. On the other hand, I had some people telling me that I needed to go in another direction. I was confused. I was scared I was going to mess up. I could not sit still. After several weeks of agonizing prayer, I knew something needed to be done.

I went down to a pond north of the house and climbed up on a rock that I had played on as a child. From this vantage point there was a break in the trees where I could look up into the sky. With eyes wide open, I stood on the rock, looked up into the heavens, and poured my heart out to God. My prayer was something like: "Father, I need an answer, and I need it now. I am torn between two opinions about my life. I have people telling me that I am called to preach, and I have other people telling me I need to move away and do something else. I don't know what to do. Please talk to me!" At that point I simply closed my eyes and bowed my head. No sooner than my chin hit my chest, I saw a mental picture of a Bible that I kept in the headboard of my bed. It was open, and all I could read was the page number in the left-hand corner—page 614.

Without hesitation, I ran to the house, back to my room, and shut the door. I grabbed the Bible and turned to page 614. The opening verse on that page read:

> And the LORD turned to him and said, "Go in this might of yours and save Israel from the hand of Midian; do not I send you?" And he said to him, "Please, Lord, how can I save Israel? Behold, my clan is the weakest in Manasseh, and I am the least in my father's house." And the LORD said to him, "But I will be with you, and you shall strike the Midianites as one man." And he said to him, "If now I have found favor in your eyes, then show me a sign that it is you who speak with me." (Judges 6:14–17)

As I sat there reading that passage, it really hit home. There was the call to preach, but there was more. Gideon identified himself as being from a poor family and being the least in his father's house. While my parents were not poor, I was! I was also the least in my father's house in the sense that I was the youngest and the least successful. As if that were not enough, I read more.

> Then Gideon said to God, "If you will save Israel by my hand, as you have said, behold, I am laying a fleece of wool on the threshing floor. If there is dew on the fleece alone, and it is dry on all the ground, then I shall know that you will save Israel by my hand, as you have said." And it was so. When he rose early next morning and squeezed the fleece, he wrung enough dew from the fleece to fill a bowl with water. Then Gideon said to God, "Let not your anger burn against me; let me speak just once more. Please let me test just once more with the fleece. Please let it be dry on

the fleece only, and on all the ground let there be
dew." And God did so that night; and it was dry
on the fleece only, and on all the ground there
was dew. (Judges 6:36–40)

I sat down and prayed, "Father, thank you for such a quick
answer—such a thorough answer. Now to be sure of this, a
confirmation if You will, I'm going to put out a fleece. If this is
a true calling, You will open a place for me to preach without
my asking for it. Someone will open a pulpit because you told
them to. In Jesus' name, amen." I never said a word about this to
anyone, and I was at peace from that moment on.

Three days later I went into the church to talk with Pastor
John and return some books he had loaned me. We spent a
couple of hours talking and praying together. As I was leaving,
John stopped me and said, "I almost forgot. I have to be out of
town the first Wednesday night of April, and I have you written
down to preach. You can't get out of it, because you're the only
one available." I sat back down and told John my story. He just
nodded his head and smiled. Confirmation!

I spent the next three weeks trying to write sermons and
had several outlines, but nothing definite. I found I could not
close a single sermon. This being my first time at preaching, I
was becoming frustrated. The day came for me to preach, and I
had nothing to say. I will admit, I was scared. I went to see my
mentor, Cliff, because he would know what to do. As I walked
into his house, I told him, "I have to preach tonight, and I have
nothing to say." He smiled and said, "Praise the Lord!" I looked
at him and said it again: "I have nothing to say tonight!" Again
he smiled and said, "Praise the Lord!" I asked him, "Are you
listening to me? I have to preach tonight, and I have nothing to
say!" He snapped back with a smile, "I heard you and answered

you. I said 'Praise the Lord.' You're not listening to me. You have nothing to say right now because we are not going to hear from you tonight, but from the Lord!'"

A bit later a friend of Cliff's came over, and he told her, "Steve's preaching tonight but he has nothing to say." She looked at me and said, "Praise the Lord!" She then encouraged me and prayed "that words may be given to me in opening my mouth boldly to proclaim the mystery of the gospel, for which I am an ambassador in chains, that I may declare it boldly, as I ought to speak" (Ephesians 6:19–20). Cliff's final comments were, "I want you to go home, put on your suit, grab your Bible and go to church. The Lord will take care of the rest." And I went home.

As instructed, I got dressed, grabbed my Bible, went to church, and sat in the front row, waiting for my turn. The worship leader came and asked if I was ready, and I said, "No. I have nothing to say." He looked at me and said, "What!" "I have nothing to say," I repeated. He looked dazed and confused.

When church started, he explained to the crowd what I had shared. He then asked for everyone to gather around and pray for me, that God would help me. He went on with the service, and with about fifteen minutes remaining, he asked me to come up and, if anything, just talk about what I was going through.

I stepped up to the pulpit, opened my Bible, and read from the text. The passage that had been opened to me was Matthew 18:1–11, which talks about receiving the kingdom as little children and not causing the little ones to sin. That was quite a text for my very first sermon. After reading the text, I froze. My knees locked, my heart started racing, I started shaking, and I could not make eye contact with the congregation. My mentor told me later that if I could have found the lever for an escape hatch, I would have pulled it.

Without raising my head, I looked over my glasses to see the crowd. Most people were just sitting there smiling, patiently waiting for me to say something. I looked at my grandmother, and she was obviously praying under her breath, as her mouth was moving and her eyes were closed. I then looked at my mentor. He was sitting there with his hands folded in his lap, a pleasant smile on his face, and he seemed to glow. Except for Cliff and my grandmother, I do not think anyone expected what was about to happen, especially not me.

All of a sudden, I felt something shoot through me. My knees unlocked and I stepped up to the pulpit and locked my right boot heel into a ledge on the pulpit (an action that my mother said always happened when I was fixing to get wound up and start preaching). I looked out over the crowd with no fear of any person in attendance. The words started coming like a flood! I saw every reaction possible upon the faces of my listeners: joy, surprise, shock, and fear. It stopped as abruptly as it started.

I closed my Bible and returned to my seat in the front row. The worship leader scrambled to close the service. As I sat there, many people came by to thank me for the message and to praise the Lord for what He was doing in and through me. When the crowd died down, I saw my mentor looking at me with a very solemn expression, and he quietly said, "How long will you doubt?" Then he walked away.

While there are many things I can glean through this story, the point I want to make is that God honors boldness. The woman with the issue of blood boldly pushed through a crowd to touch His robe and received her healing (Luke 8:40–48). Blind Bartimaeus refused to be denied as he cried out louder than the crowd's rebukes, "Jesus, Son of David, have mercy on me for I want to see!" (Mark 10:46–52 paraphrased), and he received his sight. I needed an answer to a prayer, and I went boldly to the throne of grace, seeking help. I received not only the answer to my first question, but so much more. If you are in need of help in the midst of a desperate situation, go boldly before your Father, and make your request known. He will answer you.

I Know but You Keep
Your Peace

Several years ago my family became embroiled in a situation
involving another family. Without giving any details, in order
to protect all other parties, let me just say that things got rather
heated. The hard part was that my family did a good thing
during a difficult time, and the other Christian family lashed
out in anger. Not only did this hurt my family, but it made
me angry. Although I knew the other family reacted out of
frustration, it angered me that they would act that way. My
anger was so intense that it felt like a hot knife digging deep
into my heart.

I was scheduled to preach on Wednesday evening, and
I knew if I did not deal with this anger it would affect the
service. I went to my room, got on my knees, and began to
pray: "Father, I need to get this burning anger out of my heart.
If I don't, my attitude won't be right to preach, and I'll end up
lashing out at someone. What do I do? How do I handle this?
Please remove this pain!" Instantly, my mind was led to read
2 Kings 2:1-5. At that time I had only a King James Bible, so
the language is old. If I'd had one of the newer translations
with more modern English, I might have understood the text

quicker and easier. Maybe the journey is what teaches the lesson.

2 Kings 2:1–5 is the story of when Elijah was about to be taken from this earth. He and his protégé, Elisha, were walking down the road together. In two separate places the sons of the prophets came out and said to Elisha, "Knowest thou that the LORD will take away thy master from thy head today?" And each time Elisha replied, "Yea, I know it; hold ye your peace." So I pondered the words, "Yes, I know it; hold your peace."

The first comment that was made was easy to understand. Just as Elisha told the prophets "I know," so the Lord was telling me, "I know all about this. I know what caused this. I know why everyone acted as they did. I know why you are angry, and I know the outcome. I know how this is all going to work out." So I rested in the comment that God knew my problem, but the burning knife was still stinging in my heart.

I moved on to the next comment. "Hold ye your peace." I rolled that around in my mind for a while to no avail. Then I got spiritual. I remembered that Jesus was my peace (Jehovah-Shalom). Therefore, I was to keep my eyes on Jesus, and everything would be okay. But the burning never stopped. I kept thinking this through, and it hit like a bolt from the blue. To "keep your peace" was another way of saying "be quiet."

I put all of the comments together, and I knew what God was saying. He was telling me that He knew all about the problem and that He was working things out, but He needed me to shut up. The moment I accepted what He was saying, I felt the burning knife slip from my heart, and a deep, quiet peace settled in. Over the next few days, I refused to get involved in any conversations about it. My sermon preparation came easily, and I had a great time preaching on Wednesday night.

The rest of this event culminated on Sunday morning. Following church that morning, the other family involved in the crisis came up to me and said, "We want to let you know that we have been on vacation the last few days and had a miserable time because of the way things happened over the past few days. So we have gone around to every member of the family; we want to apologize for our behavior. Can you forgive us?" Naturally, the answer was yes. So the Lord worked everything out.

When you are facing those situations in life that bring confusion and pain, fall on your knees and cry out to Him. He will come with an answer. The answer may seem obscure at first, but stay with Him and He will fully illuminate the situation. His answer will probably change you first. While He is changing you, He will also be working on the other parties involved. He will bring a resolution to the situation that will bring good for us and glory to His name.

Section V
The Voice of God

In this section I want to share a few stories of how God has spoken to me in order to reveal Himself to me and make His presence known in my life. Yes, I have heard the voice of God. I have not only heard the still, small voice deep within me; I have also heard His audible voice.

I know this is a controversial subject, even among believers, as many declare that God does not speak audibly. For the majority of the body of Christ, the belief is that God speaks to people in various forms, such as His written word, our thoughts, our circumstances, or the words spoken by others. The truth is, He does speak to us through each one of the aforementioned methods. If we even admit to hearing the voice of God, we say that we only heard a still, small voice from deep within.

The nonbeliever will claim that hearing voices is a direct result of mental illness, schizophrenia, suggestive coercion, or some type of hallucinogen or medication. Yet they themselves will do things based upon something that was in their minds. They will use language like "something told me" and words like *intuition*. Because they are nonbelievers, they cannot or will not admit to the possibility that God may be speaking to them.

When talking to those who have never heard the audible voice of God, it is difficult at best to describe what we have heard. For those of us who have heard the voice, we find it difficult to explain, because it is not something we have conjured up; He speaks on His time when we least expect it. It is also difficult to find the words that adequately describe what we heard. On the few occasions such as mentioned in this section, the voice was strong and authoritative, yet gentle and peaceful. It was a voice like no other.

May 3, 1987

The weekend of May 3, 1987, was a tumultuous three days. That weekend turned out to be a major turning point in my life. That weekend would mark the end of my old way of life and the beginning of the new. The weekend began with a traumatic event but ended in triumph.

I knew there were problems in the relationship with the young woman I had been seeing. I could sense that she was pulling away, but I was determined to hold on to her. On Friday I called and asked if I could come over, and she said no. I heard her rejection but refused to accept it. Like a fool, I went to her house anyway. Her ten-year-old step-sister came out and told me that the lady did not want to see me, but I went in anyway. I sat there for several minutes, and I was totally ignored by everyone. I finally wised up and left. That was the end.

I was angry. So I got together with a friend, and we got drunk. The drinking did not help, because I only grew more angry. Later that night, as I was heading home, a friend I shared in common with the lady needed a ride home. First she commented that she had never seen me this way before. She asked what was wrong. I unloaded every barrel I had. The friend was shocked about the way things had occurred but indicated that she knew it was coming. After dropping her off, I went home. I went to bed but slept very little.

Saturday came and the anger gave way to the hurt and the pain of yet another loss in my life. I moped around the house all day. I went for several walks on the dirt road out by our house. I tried to eat but had no appetite. I just kept replaying the last night's events in my head. I went to town that evening but came home early. I was exhausted, but I could not relax. I decided to take a couple of sleeping pills. Usually, half a pill would knock me out. Not this night. I wrestled the bed all night as the events continued to roll through my mind.

Sunday morning came. I got up and headed to the kitchen for a cup of coffee. My mom was at the sink; she looked in my direction and said, "You look like you've been run over by a Mack truck." I was not in a joking mood, so I fired back, "Yeah, and I feel like it, too!" She looked into my eyes and said, "Why don't you go to church with me?" I glared at her and asked, "Do you honestly think that I would want to serve a God who treats people the way I have been treated? I mean, people at your church do some mean things and still have everything they want, but I try to be nice and I get this. You're crazy." I walked away and she went to church.

Later that morning I decided to go take my usual walk down to the neighbor's house and back, one mile round-trip. It was already getting to be a hot, windy morning. I walked to the end of the road, turned around, and walked back. Normally, I would try to talk out my problems in order to get the thoughts out of my head. Oftentimes this helped me sort things out. That morning I took the entire walk and never said a word. Apart from the sound of me kicking at pieces of gravel, there was nothing but silence.

When I got back to my house, I stood in the middle of the road and asked, "What am I supposed to do?" From over my left shoulder I heard a voice that was so clear, so strong and yet so gentle, say, "Go to church." That voice was so real that I actually turned to see who was there, and when I saw no one, I sarcastically asked, "Do what?" Again I heard that same voice simply say, "Go to church." I stood there for a few minutes and then whispered, "That is the most sound advice I have heard in a long time." I went into the house, cleaned up, and went to church.

Several weeks before, I had gone into a motel room with the same young woman who had dumped me on Friday. As I have talked about in an earlier chapter, in that motel the Bible was left open to a message of judgment as the Scripture she pointed out said, "Let marriage be held in honor among all, and let the marriage bed be undefiled, for God will judge the sexually immoral and adulterous" (Hebrews 13:4 KJV). That morning at church, Pastor John Henry talked about the mercy, the grace, and the forgiveness of God toward sinners. I went back to the church for a singing that night, and every song spoke of God's love for me. At ten o'clock that night, Mom called Pastor John, and he came out in a terrible thunderstorm just to pray with me. I mumbled my way through the Sinner's Prayer as I asked Jesus to come into my heart.

I walked Pastor John out to his car and stood on the driveway as he left. I looked back east toward Tulsa, and I could see the backside of the thunderstorm that had just passed through our area. I looked above and saw that there were still clouds, but they were quickly clearing out, revealing a night sky full of beautiful stars. As I look back upon that night, that scene was significant. As I watched the storm moving out of our area, I could sense the storm in my heart giving way to a calming peace.

In the story of the prodigal son, we read where the young man was heading home on a dirt road. When he got close to home, his father saw him and started running toward him. In my case, I was heading home on a dirt road, and my heavenly Father saw me. I cannot say He came running, but He was sure standing there with open arms, waiting for my return. Whether you are the wandering child or have one in your family, know for sure that while such a one walks a dangerous road, the heavenly Father is standing, watching the horizon, waiting for their return. When they do, He runs to them and wraps them up in His wonderful love.

The Preacher in My Head

I remember when I first prayed the Sinner's Prayer, the night of May 3, 1987. I would hear this preacher in my head when I tried to sleep. Many nights were spent with no sleep as I lay there listening to this voice. The messages were strong and pointed, more often filled with Scriptures. No matter how hard I tried to silence the voice in order to get some rest, it was relentless in its presentation of truth. Some nights required that I would get out of bed and unload my mind onto paper. The problem was that I could not write as fast as the thoughts flowed.

I was taking a class in drafting and design in Tulsa, in order to find a new line of work due to my disabilities. The assignments were mentally tough, so I needed to concentrate. There was one day that was publicly embarrassing, to say the least. I was working away when the voice decided it wanted to have a conversation with me. I was trying to get my assignment done, but the voice had other plans. Finally, out of frustration, I blurted out, "Could you please be quiet! I'm trying to concentrate!" It was then that I looked up and saw that the two classmates who sat facing me were looking at me as if to say, "Who are you talking to?" I then tried to explain my situation to them. I told them that I was not talking to them, but rather I was trying to silence all of the voices in my head.

I think they understood, but to this day they probably think I am nuts! I still laugh about that moment.

When I went to Alabama in November of 1987, I was still hearing the voice of the preacher in my head. One Saturday night, November 13, 1987, as I lay there trying to sleep, the preacher began quoting the command of Jesus, "You must be born again." I went to church that morning with friends, as usual. Sunday night they gave an altar call, and I went forward to pray. A man I barely knew knelt beside me and quoted Romans 10:8–11: "But what does it say? 'The word is near you, in your mouth and in your heart' [that is, the word of faith that we proclaim)]; because, if you confess with your mouth that Jesus is Lord and believe in your heart that God raised him from the dead, you will be saved. For with the heart one believes and is justified, and with the mouth one confesses and is saved. For the Scripture says, 'Everyone who believes in him will not be put to shame.'"

I was under the impression that I was already saved, but I prayed with the man. I publicly confessed that Jesus was who He said He was and made sure that I put my trust in Him. I did not feel anything at the moment, but I remember later feeling as if the weight of the world had been lifted from my shoulders. Was I born again on May 3, 1987, or on November 15, 1987? I do not know. I know that each of the nights was extremely significant in my life. They are nights that I will never forget.

Go Talk to Her

Many times during speaking engagements, as well as in this writing, I have shared the story of the night I walked into a Tulsa motel with a young woman I was not married to, only to find a Bible left open to Hebrews 13:4: "Let marriage be held in honor among all, and let the marriage bed be undefiled, for God will judge the sexually immoral and adulterous." (Hebrews 13:4). On numerous occasions after telling this story, people have come up to me and asked, "What happened to the young woman in the story? Did you marry her?" No, I did not marry her. In fact, the tailspin I went into after that night was enough to drive her away. Some have put her down for not sticking with me through the rough times. Do not blame her. I don't. She had to fight for her own survival and sanity, so she left.

Several weeks after I was saved, I was out on the farm cleaning off a trailer. She drove by the house, heading down to the house of a mutual friend. As she drove by, I looked down, trying to act like I did not see her. After she passed, I heard that same voice I had heard just weeks before on that very same road, when the speaker told me, "Go to church." This time the voice simply said, "Go talk to her." I looked around to see who was nearby, and I saw that I was alone. A few seconds later the voice said again, "Go talk to her." I was terrified. I thought to myself, "I wouldn't know what to say." I had not yet learned to trust the voice, nor had I learned the truth that in that moment it would not have been me talking, but the Lord talking to her through me. So, my immature faith took control, I went back to work, and I grieved the Holy Spirit in that moment.

I have never seen the young woman since, nor have I spoken to her. I have learned that through a series of events she went into a coma a couple of years ago. From what I have learned about her lifestyle, she had not changed or made a profession of faith in Jesus Christ. I must admit that I live with some guilt that I am working through right now. That guilt involves the question, "If I had obeyed the voice that morning, spoken to her, would she have responded to the Lord's invitation as I did? Would it have altered the course of history, thus preventing this tragic state she is in now? Would she be fine today, living an abundant life?" God only knows.

My point is this: I have to learn to listen to the voice, even when it seems the directions are ludicrous. My obedience in the least matter has eternal consequences.

Just Trust Me

The year 1987 was a rough one. Over the course of several months, I had lost everything I considered valuable.

In February of that year, I had surgery on my left shoulder, which left my remaining arm incapacitated for several weeks. There I realized what disability really meant. My mother had to comb my hair for me for several weeks, as I could not raise my arm above my shoulder or move my neck.

In March, due to the inability to get around by myself, depression began to set in; my sense of worth as a man was gone. I was no longer able to care for myself, at age twenty-seven. All I did was sit around and stare at the walls.

In April I had gall bladder surgery, which further enhanced my inability to do anything. The six-inch scar had torn open, draining fluids for several weeks. Because of the bandages I had to wear and the pain in my side, I was still unable to get out and work, adding to my depression and feelings of worthlessness.

In May the one woman I thought was true to me walked out of my life. At the time that was a devastating blow. I responded to her actions by getting drunk on a Friday night and taking sleeping pills on Saturday night. That Sunday morning I was led to attend church, first by my mother's invitation and then by a divine encounter. I went back to church that evening. Around 10:30

that night, I accepted Jesus as my savior. Things were supposed to change; but the losses continued.

In June I surrendered my hay business to the Lord in search of His will for my life. My main tractor broke down and could not be repaired for several weeks, costing me my largest contracts, and the entire business was gone.

In July I surrendered my drafting classes to the Lord, again to search for His will in my life. Within a few days my left hand became so weak I could not hold a pencil. After several days of effort, I realized that I had to let the classes go.

In August I had to sell my one last possession—my truck. With all the other debts I had, I could not pay the note on the truck and had to let it go.

In September I was notified by the state of Oklahoma that my monthly disability check was being cut off, because they no longer considered me disabled. No more income. It took several months to prove to the state that I was still disabled and had no source of income.

I went to church on a Wednesday night in October, and I remember sitting in the back row next to my mother. Since she played an instrument, that never happened. As the service went on, my best friend's wife, Kari, got up and announced that they would be leaving Oklahoma and taking a new job in Alabama. As I sat there listening to this news, I thought, "Are you kidding me? After all that I have been through, I am now losing my best friend? What am I supposed to do now?" At that moment I heard a voice say, "Just trust me." I turned to my mom and asked if she said anything, to which she replied, "No." I sat back, looked straight ahead, and listened. Again the voice said, "Just trust me." I quietly whispered, "Okay." At that moment I was filled with a peace that, as the Scriptures say, "surpasses all understanding" and a joy that is "unspeakable and full of glory."

Go Home with Him

One Sunday evening I was walking out of church when I heard the voice say, "Follow him home." I had come to recognize the voice, so I looked around to see whom the voice was talking about. There were several people around, so I was not sure what to do. When my eyes fell on a retired preacher named Cliff Funk, the voice again said, "Follow him home." I walked up to Cliff and said, "I'm not sure why, but I feel like I am supposed to come over and talk with you tonight." He looked at me, smiled, and said, "I know. Here's my address and number. Give me about thirty minutes to change and eat. Then we'll talk." As I stood there in the parking lot watching him walk away, the thought crossed my mind, "He knows all about this. He had this note ready and in his hand. What does he know that I don't?"

After I arrived, we took a seat on the front porch. We talked for a long time. We talked so long, in fact, that the sun was long gone and the porch was dark. We left the light off so we would not attract any bugs. The only light we had was the warm glow coming through the window, which put him in an unusual light. He shared a few things about himself but mainly asked me about my life. Finally we stopped talking, and he just looked at me. He leaned forward, pushed his glasses up with each index finger (I soon discovered this was his trademark move when he was about to say something very important), and said, "I'm not going to prophesy over you … yes, I will!" The words he spoke to me in those next few moments were very sobering.

"You are called to preach. You have been created to preach. You have tried everything to make money and a career, but you have failed because you were created for the purpose of preaching. But you were not created to be the typical preacher. You were cut from a different mold. You were created to preach a different message. You were created to preach a strong, pointed message. You were created for a ministry that is not always accepted but is necessary to the health of the church. I know this because you were cut from the same mold as me.

"You will be held to a different lifestyle. While your preacher friends will be free to do certain things, you will not. Do not judge them for this, because the Lord Himself has given them the freedom to enjoy these things and still be in His perfect will. But you will not be free to do certain things. Your ministry will appear difficult and oftentimes hard. You must remember to trust the Lord for everything. He is the Potter, you are the clay, and He has formed you for this purpose."

I am not sure I was ready to hear those words. First, I wanted to stay on the farm. I told the Lord I would do anything in the church that He wanted, just let me keep farming. Second, I was scared to death to stand in front of a crowd of people and speak. I almost gave myself an ulcer while attending a trade school, for fear that I would have to take a public speaking class the next trimester. Third, I just flat out did not want to be a preacher. Couple those thoughts with the words Cliff just spoke, and I definitely wanted to shrink back from following the Lord.

Cliff was not lying that night. My preaching ministry has been difficult, to say the least. I have tried to write those nice pastoral messages that all my friends shared, but the sermons seemed to fall to the floor, flop like a fish, and burst into flames. On top of that, I always felt as if I had wasted the Lord's and the people's time with such outlines. When I did what I felt led to do, I found myself preaching provocative messages that would agitate some and bless others. When I preached these messages, I always felt fulfilled and at peace with the Lord.

Do I regret hearing the voice that night? A voice that sent me to a man's house where I heard what to expect in the years to come? Not one bit. For one, I was introduced to my greatest mentor, Cliff Funk. While we talked about many things the next two years, his focus was always on obedience to the Lord and loving the ones that seemed most unlovable. I miss him so much and would give anything to sit at his feet one more night.

Section VI
The Dreams

In this section, I want to share a few stories of how God used dreams in order to make His presence known in my life and to give me direction. Of the five dreams I share, the first two a generic in nature, giving me direction and encouragement for specific areas of life. The last three dreams that I share, the dark dreams, came as a sequence , one following after the other, yet connected in the sense that they shared the same message. On the day of Pentecost, Peter echoed words spoken by the prophet Joel centuries ago: "And it shall come to pass afterward, that I will pour out my Spirit on all flesh; your sons and your daughters shall prophesy, your old men shall dream dreams, and your young men shall see visions. Even on the male and female servants in those days I will pour out my Spirit" (Joel 2:28–29). God says that He will speak to His people in a dream, and He will make Himself known in a vision. He uses both of these instruments to draw us into His purposes.

In this modern age, believers and nonbelievers alike are skeptical of God speaking to them through dreams. We like to talk to others about our dreams. But we are usually quick at brushing off a strange dream. We want to blame it on the food we had for dinner or some television program we watched the night before. Admitting to the fact that God may be speaking to us in a dream is something we do not readily do.

God uses dreams not only to direct us into His plans and purposes but also to warn men of troubles that will come.

Job 33:14–18 states: "For God speaks in one way, and in two, though man does not perceive it. In a dream, in a vision of the night, when deep sleep falls on men, while they slumber on their beds, then he opens the ears of men and terrifies them with warnings, that he may turn man aside from his deed and conceal pride from a man; he keeps back his soul from the pit, his life from perishing by the sword." Such is the case of the dark dreams that I share in this section.

Does this mean that all dreams are divine in their nature? Probably not. But that is still no reason to discount the fact that God is speaking to us.

The Running Man

In this dream, I saw myself constantly on the move. It was cool, because I saw myself with two arms and running through a maze of city streets and alleys. I saw myself using the pipes above my head to propel myself farther and in different directions. I was always on the move. There was something that looked like rolled-up newspapers stuck in my hip pocket. After a time of running, I came up to a guy and showed him the papers I carried, and then we shook hands. I took off again. Shortly after, I came to a second guy. Once again I showed him the papers, and he backed off a bit and looked uneasy. I stepped forward and showed him the papers again. He then smiled and shook my hand. I took off a third time. Then I came to another guy. As before, I pulled the papers from my pocket and showed them to the third guy. He hit me in the face and knocked me down! I got up and showed him the papers again, and he acted as if he were going to hit me again. He was angry! I backed away, pointing at him, and then took off running. The dream ended.

I could not shake that dream the next day. It was replayed in my mind three times that night, each time the same. I was exhausted the next morning, and my legs felt as if I had been running all night. I went over to my mentor's house and shared the dream with him. We prayed for wisdom and understanding. As we continued to talk, we both came to the same conclusion as to the meaning of the dream.

I was the runner. The rolled-up paper I carried and showed to all three men was the message of the gospel. The constant moving was the urgency and necessity of getting the message out to everyone I could. The reactions of the three men represent the basic reactions that can be expected when the gospel is preached. The first man accepted the message without hesitation and thanked me with a handshake. The second man was not as quick to accept the message. In fact, he needed more persuasion. After more presentation he too accepted the message and thanked me with a handshake. The third man hated the message and the messenger. That is why he hit me! When I tried to press the matter home, his anger grew. But I pulled back, gave him a warning, and headed off.

Through this dream, God has taught me several things. First, He used this dream as a call to preach the gospel. Over the past twenty-five years, I may not have been in a pulpit, but somehow my conversations with people always get back to the message of the gospel. The second thing God taught me was the urgency of the hour. Being on the run implied that we need to get the message of God's salvation in Christ to as many people as quickly as we can. The third thing God taught me was the reactions I would get when I shared the message of grace. I have had people latch on to the message without hesitation. Although I have never been hit like the runner in the dream, I have had people get angry with me over the message.

The hour is late and we need to get the message out to as many as we can as quickly as we can.

The People, the Hands, the Plain, and the Curtain

During my first year as a Christian, I was facing what I saw as overwhelming circumstances. These circumstances were the kind that would cause me to have the cold sweats at night. I would toss and turn as images of the matters at hand would press in on my mind. During the daytime, my stomach would twist into knots, and I found it hard to get anything done. These circumstances were crippling.

In the dream I was standing in a large crowd of people. Some of the people there I recognized. The majority of the crowd, however, had no facial features. Instead their faces appeared as fuzzy, white orbs. As I stood there looking at the crowd, they all turned my way and began pressing in on me. I thought I was going to be crushed by them. I was just about to panic. Suddenly, a set of large hands came down from above and settled like a wall between me and the crowd. Then the hands moved away from me, sweeping the crowd away.

Once the crowd was gone, I saw before me a large, smooth, deep blue expanse that reached as far as the eye could see. Above the expanse was the most beautiful blue sky I had ever seen. I noticed a black object off in the distance. I began to move toward it to see what it was. My intentions were thwarted, however, when a curtain began to drop down from above. As the curtain got closer to the ground, I got down on my stomach to see what the object was. I became frustrated when the curtain obscured my vision.

When I awoke the next morning, I pondered the dream. I did not need any help interpreting this dream. The crowd represented all of the circumstances that were pressing in on me. The hands belonged to the Lord. As we learn to trust Him, He sweeps away the problems and leaves before us a clear path. The object in the distance is what He has prepared for us. The curtain coming down was God's way of saying it was there but I was not ready yet. I still cannot explain what my object was or why I was not allowed to see it. I still pray for the curtain to be lifted so I can have access to what God has prepared for me.

The Dancing Man

This is the first in the sequence of the three dark dreams I experienced. I did not realize that I was flirting with disaster. I allowed myself to get involved in a practice that, if continued, would lead to serious problems. Before you try to figure out my personal situation, look at your life and see if there is something you are flirting with.

In this dream I saw myself standing with several other people. We were watching this little man dance around. He was quite colorful in his dress, and he had an inviting smile on his face. There was no music. He simply danced around in small circles, using his hands to beckon us closer. I decided to let him get closer to me. I found him quite entertaining. When I was close enough, he pulled out two very sharp knives and began slashing at me. As I tried to get away, I found myself tripping over the edge of a dark precipice. When he got close enough, he pushed me over the edge, and I fell into the bottomless pit.

When the third dream sequence ended, I woke up scared. I was breathing heavily and sweating profusely. I sat there in the dark trying to understand why I'd had such a dream. I am ashamed to admit that I did not understand that the Lord was trying to send me a warning. I went back to bed and slept the rest of the night. While I did not understand the dream at first, it lodged deep within my mind.

Has God been trying to warn you of something that you have been flirting with? An action? An attitude? A relationship? A career in a field that He is not pleased with? He will speak in the night with strong warnings, because He loves us.

Death in the Darkness

This is the second in the sequence of the dark dreams. This is the only dream I have had that did not follow the pattern of three times in the same night, occurring instead over a series of three nights. This dream was slightly different in that the message was the same, but the presentation of the message was slightly different each time.

In the first two dreams, I found myself in a large building that was quite gloomy. On the left side of the building was a wide ramp that led to an upper area that was pitch black. Although I felt apprehension, my curiosity got the best of me, and I began to make my way up the ramp. I could feel a coldness, but I was still drawn to the darkness. When I reached a certain place on the ramp, a black misty figure flew out of the darkness and swallowed me up. When that occurred, I was filled with a deep sense of terror and dread. Then I was gone.

In the third dream of the sequence, I found myself on an elaborate stairwell. It was the kind of stairwell that would be found in older buildings. There were two flights of stairs going up to the next floor, one on each side of the room. The stairs were joined together by a landing. On one side of the landing was a railing and one the other there was a single stairwell going up to the next floor. If you looked over the railing, you would see a bottomless pit. At the top of the single stairway was a small door. It was nothing special in appearance, but it had an appeal to it. Again curiosity prevailed. I climbed the stairs, turned the knob, and began to open the door. Without warning, the same black misty figure from the previous dreams came flying through the door. The figure swallowed me up and took me over the edge into the bottomless pit. As before, I was filled with a deep sense of terror and dread.

When this dream ended, I woke up scared. As with the dancing man, I was breathing heavily and sweating profusely. I sat there in the dark trying to understand why I'd had such a dream. I am ashamed to admit that I still did not understand that the Lord was trying to send me a warning. I went back to bed and slept the rest of the night. While I did not understand the dream, as with the first dream, it lodged deep within my mind.

Before you judge me for my apparent cluelessness, let me say that Satan's deception blinds us from seeing the truth. Even people who go to church and claim to walk with the Lord have been deceived into believing a lie. At that point, I had been blinded by the Enemy. I could not see the warnings.

Left Behind!

This is the third dream in the sequence of the dark dreams. I found myself in a very large crowd that was gathered in what looked like an entry into an airplane terminal. Most of the crowd wore blank faces, just white orbs, though I did recognize my children. I realized that it was just about time for departure, and I was scrambling to get my children through the doors. I was in a panic, because I could not get close to my children. Then the doors were shut, and I saw my youngest walking away from me, waving good-bye. At that moment, I realized that I was being left behind! I ran up to the doors, but they were locked. Horror swept over me at the thought of being left behind.

As with the other two dream in the series, I woke up terrified. I was breathing heavily and sweating profusely. I sat there in the dark trying to understand why I'd had such a dream. Then my eyes were opened. The Lord had used these dreams to tell me that I was on my way to being left behind. For several weeks the guilt was overwhelming, and the fear of being lost forever was too real. I was drawn to Psalm 51, where I cried out

> Have mercy on me, O God, according to your
> steadfast love; according to your abundant

mercy blot out my transgressions. Wash me thoroughly from my iniquity, and cleanse me from my sin! For I know my transgressions, and my sin is ever before me. Against you, you only, have I sinned and done what is evil in your sight, so that you may be justified in your words and blameless in your judgment. Create in me a clean heart, O God, and renew a right spirit within me. Cast me not away from your presence, and take not your Holy Spirit from me. Restore to me the joy of your salvation, and uphold me with a willing spirit.

I struggled to find the forgiveness that I so desperately sought. I knew that the Scriptures said that if we confess our sins, He is faithful and just to forgive us of our sin and cleanse us from all iniquity. I knew this was true, but the words were not soaking in. I wrote to three trusted friends and openly confessed my sin. They encouraged me greatly, but the guilt was still there. Then, out of the blue, a friend from way back started sending me a series of songs, emails, and text messages stating that God had told her to tell me that He was still with me and that He was beginning a new work in me.

If you are flirting with anything that you know the Lord has warned you about, flee with all haste. Be very careful, because your enemy, the Devil, comes as an angel of light, drawing you into his hidden darkness.

Section VII
The Healings

In this section I want to share a few stories of God making His presence known in my life through healings and deliverances. These are the times when you have a specific need in your body or mind and you ask God for help, and He answers in an unusual manner. We can use the terms *miracle, healing, deliverance, sign,* or *wonder,* but technically it is all the same. It is a time when God touches you and the problem simply goes away.

This in itself can be a controversial subject even among believers. The body of Christ is deeply divided upon this subject. At one extreme there are those who believe that it is God's will that everyone be healed. They believe that all it takes is a little bit of faith. On the other hand, there are those who believe that the age of miracles has passed. They believe that miracles performed by Jesus and the apostles were solely for the purpose of establishing the gospel message. Now that the message is established, there is no more need of miraculous validation. Scattered between the two extremes is a myriad of beliefs upon the subject; so vast are the beliefs that it would require more room than I have here to describe them.

As for me, I believe God still heals. I believe it is God's nature to heal, as one of His names is Jehovah-Ropheka, meaning "the Lord is healing." He says of Himself in Exodus 15:26, "I am the Lord God that heals you." I believe healing is a part of the plan of salvation, as Isaiah 53:5 says: "By His stripes we are healed." I believe that healing did not stop with the end of the apostolic age but continues today as each generation needs to see the message validated before them. I also believe that if Jesus healed then, He heals today, for He says, "I the LORD do not change" (Malachi 3:6), and "I am the same yesterday, today, and forever" (Hebrews 13:8).

Cold Beer and a Cigarette

Shortly after coming to Jesus, I noticed that many old habits simply fell away. My language began to change and become cleaner. My anger began giving way to peace. There were many things that changed.

I quit drinking overnight. There was no struggle; the desire simply left. In twenty-five years, I remember only one time that a cold beer looked good. I had just finished helping a friend move things into storage so he could leave for St. Louis. It was a hot day … a very hot day! Instead of paying me money, my friend took me to Steak & Ale for their nine-pepper filet and all-you-can-eat salad bar. As we sat down, I looked over at a cold beer in a frosty mug, and in my sweaty condition I said, "Boy, put a little salt in that beer, and it would taste so good right now." My friend looked at me and said to go ahead. I looked at him and said, "As tempting as that is, I have to say no for several reasons. For starters, God took away my alcoholic tendencies, and I've been clean for several years, and that is something you don't tempt. Second, I have two small boys who are trusting me to practice what I preach, so what if I came home with beer on my breath? Third, what if there is someone here who is struggling in their faith with this very issue, and they see me drink and hear me preach, and it causes them to stumble. No, a big glass of sweet tea will suit me fine!"

Now, smoking was a different animal. It had a hold on me like a pair of vise grips. I prayed. Others prayed for me. I wept and prayed. I got counseling. I tried cold turkey. I tried the gum. Five months later I was still puffing away. I would look at other people smoking and think what a nasty habit, only to put a cigarette to my lips and take a drag. What a judgmental hypocrite! I finally came to the place where enough was enough. One night my prayer time was very short but to the point. I knelt by my bed, looked up to heaven, and said, "Dear Jesus, You said that I shall know the truth, and the truth shall make me free. You said You are the truth. You said that if the Son makes me free, I am free indeed. Lord, I'm in bondage to these cigarettes. I want to be free. If You want me free, You need to break the chains of bondage, because I am too powerless. It's up to You. In Jesus' name, amen." And I went to bed.

My usual morning routine was to put on my jeans, head to the kitchen, get a cup of coffee, and grab a cigarette. It was the same routine for the past six years. The morning after my "help me quit smoking prayer," things went different. I got up at my usual time and followed the standard routine. Two hours later, I came through the kitchen and saw a pack of cigarettes on the table. It hit me: I have been up two hours and have yet to smoke a cigarette, so I lit one up. It tasted like the first cigarette I ever smoked—nasty! I put it out after one drag; then I remembered my prayer.

I went all day without a craving or withdrawal. It was easy, until five o'clock that evening. I guess I got a bit grumpy with my mom. I went and lay on a couch just off from the kitchen.

The pain was terrible. I felt like my toenails were being pulled from the inside and up through my nose. This lasted about an hour. All of a sudden, my body was filled with such a beautiful, peaceful feeling that started in my head and worked its way down to my toes. I got up and stepped into the kitchen, where my mother quipped, "I hope you're in a better mood." I looked at her, smiled, and said, "I'll never smoke another cigarette."

After ten years of smoking, and reaching a chain level of two or three packs a day, I was free. I have been smoke-free for twenty-five years. I have never had a craving, a nicotine fit, or any type of withdrawal. When I first quit, I would hear a voice in my head (not the same voice I wrote about in another section) ask me, "Wouldn't a cigarette be great right now?" I would smile and say, "Yeah, it would. But I don't want one." And off I would go.

Jesus came to set the captive free, and whoever He sets free is free indeed!

That Nasty Rash

I had developed a rash on my arm that was not only painful but kind of nasty to look at. I do not know to this day what it was or what brought it on; I just know that it needed to be dealt with. I was raised in a church that believes in divine healing. We believe that when a person is sick we are to follow the words written in the book of James. "Is anyone among you sick? Let him call for the elders of the church, and let them pray over him, anointing him with oil in the name of the Lord. The prayer of faith will save the one who is sick, and the Lord will raise him up. If he has committed sins, he will be forgiven. Therefore, confess your sins to one another and pray for one another, that you may be healed. The prayer of a righteous person has great power as it is working (James 5:14–16).

During the time we would gather at the altar and pray for one another, I went down and asked the elders to pray for me. They gathered around and the head elder took the oil, put some on his finger, and swabbed it across my forehead. I thought he poured out the whole bottle, because I felt it running down my nose. Those heavy elder hands fell on me, and they began to pray. They prayed their hearts out, and I knelt there in agreement. When I stood up I saw no change but accepted the prayer of faith. I went home and went to bed.

The next morning I woke up and looked at my arm. The rash was gone! My skin was as smooth as a baby's behind! There was no scar, no redness or marks of any kind! I was healed by the power of God.

The effectual fervent prayers of righteous saints availed much.

My Aching Back

There was a period of time at my home church when some of the brothers would meet once a week for a time of corporate prayer. The numbers in attendance would vary from week to week. We would sit around the room, make our prayer requests known, pray, and close with a praise chorus or two. On this one cold morning, only three of us were present. We prayed around the circle and were about to leave the prayer room. I had not mentioned it before, but my back was killing me. I could not straighten up, and I had trouble walking. So the two brothers stood there with me, and we prayed a very simple prayer of faith for healing. We then made our way downstairs, and I headed for my car. When I reached down for the door handle, I noticed the pain had gone away. I was standing up straight and strong and pain-free. I immediately shut the door and headed back into the church and found the two brothers. I looked at them, smiled, and said, "I'm healed! The pain is gone! Thought you needed to know that!" And I headed back out the door, rejoicing.

Jesus said, "Again I say to you, if two of you agree on earth about anything they ask, it will be done for them by my Father in heaven. For where two or three are gathered in my name, there am I among them" (Matthew 18:19–20).

The God of the Thumbnail

During my first year of college, I chose to live in the dorms for economic reasons. Because our college was small, our dorms looked more like a two-story motel, complete with heavy steel doors. Some of the doors, including mine, would not latch when simply pulled shut. They had to be shut *hard*. More often than not, the doors needed to be slammed.

One evening as I was heading for supper, I got my thumb stuck in the door as it was slamming shut. I do not know to this day how I managed to accomplish this, but I did and it hurt! I stepped back into the room, sat down and looked at my thumb. Within seconds it was turning colors and trying to swell. I knew it would be worse in the morning. I knew from experience that it would probably be sore and swollen, with the nail either turning black or falling off. This was not good.

I started to pray a simple prayer that went something like this, "Lord Jesus, that hurt. I need Your help. As You know, I have only one hand to do what I have to do, and a sore thumb makes things near impossible. And Lord, I start finals tomorrow, with three big essays to write over the next two days. I ask You to remove the pain, take away the swelling, and please don't let the nail fall off. Thank You. In Jesus' name, amen." Within a few moments, the pain disappeared, the swelling went down, and my thumb turned back to it's normal color. I went to the cafeteria and told my friends what happened. I even tapped the thumb on the table like a drumstick to prove there was no pain. I call it a miracle.

The next morning at coffee, a couple of friends asked about my thumb. I said there was no pain, no swelling, no discoloration. When I showed them my thumb, we all noticed that I was right about everything but one—the nail had turned black. We all have that one friend who feels the need to state the obvious. He looked at my thumb and said, "You forgot to pray about the nail turning colors, didn't you?" I went about my business of taking my final exams and had no trouble writing for several hours.

Several weeks later I received a phone call to preach at a small country church I had been to several times before. The appointed time arrived, and we began the service. We sang a few songs, took up the offering, and had a time of prayer. Then the gentleman who sang most of the specials in the church came up to the podium. Now, I do not mean to be judgmental here, but this man seemed to present himself with the attitude of "I'm in the house and everyone needs to listen to me because, after all, I'm important." I may be wrong, but that seemed to be the spirit he presented, and from the looks on faces in the crowd, others felt the same way. Before he sang, he felt like he needed to share a few words. He said, "I listen to prayer requests all the time, and I think we waste too much of God's time on trivial issues. We stub our toe, and we talk to God. We cut a finger and talk to God. We go to Him for this little thing and that little thing. What a waste of time. We need to remember that God has bigger fish to fry than to be concerned about your toe or your finger or all of the other trivial things in your life." He sang his song, strolled off the stage, sat down at the back of the church, and crossed his arms.

Then it was my turn. I felt a bit uneasy, considering the message I was about to deliver. I began by telling the crowd that it was rare for me to give my sermons a title, but I called my message for that Sunday morning "The God of the Thumbnail." Following the comments just made by the special singer, I saw many eyebrows raised, some side glances in his direction—as if looking for a reaction—and a scowl come across his face. We looked at each other for a few seconds, like two gunfighters in the middle of an Old West street. It was so quiet, you could have heard in your mind that familiar tune of Clint Eastwood's *The Good, the Bad, and the Ugly* and see tumbleweeds bouncing their way through the church. Then I drew my weapons and began delivering the ammunition God had given me.

I laid out an outline that shared the wonderful love that God has for each one of us. I talked about how God wants to pour out His blessings upon us if we will just be open to receive them. I took the listeners to the place where they heard the fact that God is not concerned only about the big things in our lives, but in every single detail. He even knows the number of hairs upon each one of our heads. That is a God of great detail and deep intimate concern for His children. That is a Father who listens to every word that comes from His child's mouth with undivided attention. I closed the message with the story of God hearing my cry concerning my busted thumb and the fact that He healed it.

As we dismissed the service and I stood at the back door shaking hands, many people came up and thanked me for reminding them of the deep care and concern the Father had for them. As for the special singer, he grumbled his way past me and refused to shake my hand.

"Humble yourselves, therefore, under the mighty hand of God so that at the proper time He may exalt you, casting all your anxieties on Him, because He cares for you" (1 Peter 5:6–7). It does not say cast some of your cares, most of your cares, or only your most pressing cares upon Him who cares for you. The Scripture says to cast *all* of your cares, *every one* of your cares, the *full range* of your cares. He wants us to bring every little detail of our lives to Him, because He cares about us, even our smashed thumbs and stubbed toes.

The Knot in My Stomach

In the late nineties, I began to experience a very painful stomach problem. It appeared that my stomach would swell, as if someone had pumped me full of air. The muscles across my stomach area would tighten up and cramp as if with an old-fashioned charley horse. The pain was intense. The only relief I seemed to find was either to throw up or to down a can of hot 7-Up and then try to belch it out. But even that did not always help. While it usually happened in the middle of the night, it did sometimes occur during the day while I was at work. The doctors had no clue, so I prayed for relief, but it never came.

One night around two o'clock in the morning, I felt the tightening start, and I sat up in bed. The first thought to cross my mind was to get up and follow my normal routine. As I was getting ready to kick off the covers, something deep inside of me changed. The following words came from deep within and went out into the darkness of the night. "Jesus cursed a tree and it died. He said I can do the same things He did. In fact, He said that if I say to a mountain, be removed, and be cast into the sea, and I don't doubt in my heart, but shall believe that those things will happen (Mark 11:23). Therefore, I am telling you, stomach pain, whatever you are, that you need to leave my body, and go back to the abyss from which you came, and touch no one on the way out of this house. In Jesus' name." The pain did not subside. It left instantly, as if it had never been there.

Several weeks later I was awakened by the old familiar tightening feeling again. Without even rolling over, I simply said, "What did I tell you? You're no longer welcome or allowed here. Leave." The pain left. Twelve years later it has never made another appearance.

"Truly, I say to you, whoever says to this mountain, 'Be taken up and thrown into the sea,' and does not doubt in his heart, but believes that what he says will come to pass, it will be done for him. Therefore I tell you, whatever you ask in prayer, believe that you have received it, and it will be yours. And whenever you stand praying, forgive, if you have anything against anyone, so that your Father also who is in heaven may forgive you your trespasses" (Mark 11:23–25).

Conclusion

In the eyes of many, this book may appear to be an exercise in vanity and ego. After all, it is 32,000 words about me. Vain and egotistical? Nothing could be further from the truth. While these are stories from my life, they are not stories about me, but rather are stories about God. They are stories about God working in my life, more often than not, in spite of me. These stories represent Immanuel moments in my life, when God made His presence known in the circumstances of my life.

I have found that writing these stories has been an exercise in personal encouragement. When I started this work, my faith in God had died down to glowing embers. It was there, but not strong. Writing these stories has helped rekindle a faith and fire in me that, once again, believes God can do exceedingly abundantly more than I could ever ask or think (Ephesians 3:20). These stories have brought me back to a place where I believe God can do the impossible.

I have found this work to be an exercise in encouragement to others as well. It is my prayer that these stories help you remember times in your own life when you knew God was present. I hope that in reading this, you not only remember your own Immanuel moments, but that you develop a hunger to seek Him more. I pray that the words of this book bring you to a place where you believe God for the miraculous—for Immanuel moments.

Immanuel—God with us!

About the Author

Following a dramatic series of events, author Steve Wheeler came to know Jesus as his personal savior in 1987. Following another series of events, Steve answered the call to the preaching ministry in 1988. He is a graduate of Mid America Christian University in Oklahoma City. He has served as Senior Pastor, Associate Pastor, and Interim Pastor of several churches in Oklahoma and Louisiana. While in college, Steve wrote a thesis for a subject he chose, completed the research, developed a survey that was mailed to pastors across the nation, and wrote a final paper that was fifty-two pages in length entitled "Power of the Pulpit." Steve has self-published one book, entitled *Forget What? The Philippian Misconception*, which is the prequel to this book. He currently resides in Mustang, Oklahoma.

References

1. Aylesworth, John, Bernie Brillstein, and Frank Peppiatt. *Gloom, Despair, and Agony on Me.* 1969.
2. Sanchez, Ricardo. *It's Not Over.* 2011.
3. *People.com.* <u>A Solitary Soul on Ice, Coach Herb Brooks Drove His Young Olympians to Glory</u>. March 10, 1980. http://www.people.com/people/archive/article/0,,20075987,00.html
4. *People.com.* <u>A Solitary Soul on Ice, Coach Herb Brooks Drove His Young Olympians to Glory</u>. March 10, 1980. http://www.people.com/people/archive/article/0,,20075987,00.html
5. *The Ten Commandments.* Dir. Cecil B. DeMille. Paramount Pictures. 1956.
6. *TeachingAmericanHistory.org.* Ashbrook Center at Ashland University. 2006-2012. http://www.teachingamericanhistory.org/library/index.asp?document=146.
7. *UN.org.* United Nations General Assembly. 11-10-2012. http://www.un.org/webcast/ga/56/statements/011110usa.htm.
8. *PBS.org.* MacNeil/Lehrer Productions. 1996-2012. http://www.pbs.org/newshour/updates/oklahoma_04-19-05.html.